ABOUT THE AUTHOR

Since 1976, Roger C. Palms has been editor of the Billy
Graham Evangelistic Association's DECISION magazine,
which is among the most widely distributed Christian period-
icals in the world. He also directs the publication of BGEA's
ALIVE! magazine. One of the most influential Christian
journalists today, Roger is the author of 14 books, including
Celebrate Life After 50 and *Enjoying the Closeness of God.*
His nightly radio program "Something For You" is broadcast
on the Skylight Satellite Network.

Bible Readings ON HOPE

This Billy Graham Evangelistic Association
edition is published by special arrangement
with the author and the original publisher,
Augsburg Publishing House.

Bible
Readings
ON
HOPE

Roger C. Palms

WORLD WIDE PUBLICATIONS
Minneapolis, Minnesota 55403

Bible Readings On Hope

Cover photo by Gary Johnson.

PREFACE

Hope!

We can't live without it. Take away hope and we will weaken, we will die. Do you have hope? Real hope? Abiding hope? Eternal hope? God offers that kind of hope to you.

We all want physical hope, good health, financial security; we also want emotional hope, peace of mind. This is human hope, and it is important, it is good. But God offers us even more than that.

God offers a deeper hope, not only for now but for always. It's called eternal hope. It lasts for now; it lasts forever. In Scripture, God tells us about that hope— how to have it and how to enjoy it every day. That hope is in Jesus Christ.

In these pages you will find refreshing, exciting biblical assurance of the hope that God offers you.

Hope like this is what you have been looking for. If you have ever said, "I wish I had hope; I want hope," then sit back and relax as you begin to explore and discover the treasures of real hope.

■ THE SOURCE OF HOPE

Ps. 39:4-7: "But now, Lord, what do I look for? My hope is in you" (v. 7).

We were having one of those after-church-in-the-narthex conversations.

"What are you working on?"

"A book about hope."

Silence, then, "You know, I can't recall ever seeing a book on hope."

"Why do you suppose that is?"

"I guess because every Christian is supposed to have it. But no one seems to be able to explain what it is that we're supposed to have."

Maybe that's because we've tended to separate hope from the source of hope, as if it's an entity in itself. Is there any hope? we ask. Do you have hope? "I hope so," someone says.

The psalmist put hope where it belongs—in God. For him hope was not something to be anticipated. His concentration wasn't in a "hope so." He said clearly, for all the generations that follow to know, "My hope is in you."

Lord, as I read this book daily, may I discover more of you, my Hope.

Determine now that each day you will go beyond a searching for hope to a deeper search for more of God. When you do, you will have hope.

■ WHY?

Ps. 42:1-5: "Why are you downcast, O my soul? Why so disturbed within me? Put your hope in God" (v. 5).

Have you talked to your soul recently? David did. He was so depressed when he wrote this psalm that he pleaded with his own soul, "Why are you downcast?"

He had been crying day and night. He couldn't even eat. His tears were his food. "Why?" he asked. And in those long, dark nights when we can't sleep and in those pain-filled days when we can't even eat, we ask that question too. When our friends try to help us, when they attempt to cheer us up or tell us to eat something and we can't, we turn to the Psalms, and David shows us the way out. "Put your hope in God," is his answer.

God is still God. God always has been and always will be. And, though all we may be able to do right now is cling to who God is and what God is, that's enough. We may not be able to praise. We may not be able to sing. We may not even be able to pray, but we can hang on to the conviction that God is God. With David we can look ahead and say, "I will yet praise God."

"Why?" isn't a bad question. It can be a necessary question because it points us past the ones who can only guess at answers and takes us to the heart of the One who is the answer.

O God, when my soul is downcast, thank you that you are there.

Remember how God has brought you through painful times before. God will do it again.

■ AGAINST ALL HOPE

Rom. 4:16-21: "Against all hope, Abraham in hope believed" (v. 18).

But that can't be; there is no hope. If anyone could have justly said that, Abraham could have. He was an old man, aged 100. His wife, Sarah, was 90 years old. But God said, "Look up at the heavens and count the stars—if indeed you can count them. So shall your offspring be" (Gen. 15:5).

We think of hope as simply a reasonable belief. We have hope if we can understand what we hope for. But Abraham believed against hope. His hope was a conviction that stood beyond hope.

God is beyond hope because God is beyond our understanding of what can be. Abraham believed, trusted, and put his faith in God who is hope beyond all human hope.

There are no limits to God, and there are no limits to hope. God is hope. This is not wishful thinking but reality, as real as God is himself. God answers our "there is no hope" doubtings. He shows us hope, a hope against hope.

 Lord, thank you that hope is more than I think it is.

If you have put strings of limitation on God today, consciously cut those strings.

■ WILL GOD ANSWER?

Song of Songs 5:1-16: "I called him but he did not answer" (v. 6).

Ask a young bride if she understands the problems that come to marriage, and she'll probably reply, "Oh, yes, I understand." But what she's probably thinking is, "Those problems will never come to us." Then they do—an argument, a misunderstanding, preoccupation, waning interest—and she finds herself saying what the young woman said in the Song of Songs, "I called him but he did not answer." Then comes the pain and the guilt—"What have I done wrong? Why doesn't he respond?" The hope she feels is an aching hope, a wondering hope. "Will he come back? Will he once again answer me when I call?"

Sometimes we transfer to God the feelings we have about human love—"Will God answer me? Has God gone away? Is God angry with me? Have I done something wrong?" Scripture says, "He will call upon me, and I will answer" (Ps. 91:15).

God isn't a recalcitrant husband. God isn't a stony wife. God is faithful to his own promise. God says, "He will call upon me, and I will answer. I will," God says. And God does.

 Thank you, Lord, for the promise that when I call you will answer.

Today practice being more sensitive to those around you whom you love.

John 10:27-29: "They shall never perish; no one can snatch them out of my hand" (v. 28).

What parent hasn't spent nights weeping over a rebellious son or daughter? We watch them bring pain to themselves even as they bring hurt to us, the parents who love them.

And we remember when they were young—professing faith, talking of their love for God, praying, giving a good confession of their belief. But now we wonder, "Will he or she return to faith?"

We watch our children, love them, yearn for them. We weigh our words lest even a gentle suggestion in love sends our young ones farther away. We agonize over the trouble our children bring upon themselves, the torment, the emotional and physical results. We watch, all the time thinking, "What might have been," or "If only."

Then we remember the promise of Jesus and we hope. It is a hope based not on what we see today or what we'll see next week. It is a hope in what may come 10 or 20 or 30 years from now. We hope because Jesus said, "They shall never perish; no one can snatch them out of my hand."

 Lord, once more I place my children in your care.

Is there a child or teenager who needs your special attention today?

WHEN THE CURTAIN FALLS

Col. 3:1-4:   "Then you also will appear with him in glory" (v. 4).

Every drama has its ending. If a play is poorly done, we sit bored or in misery, looking forward to the curtain dropping on the last act. Even when the play is delightful and we are enjoying every part of it—laughing and feeling good—we know the curtain is going to come down.

It's that way with life—good, bad, happy, sorrowful, delightful, miserable. Some day the curtain is coming down; the last act will close. Christ is coming. When he does, he will claim his own. We will appear with him in glory. Those who went Home years ago will be with him. Those still waiting for the last few lines of the last act of their life drama will be with him too. Some are ready now, waiting. He's coming, and "then you also will appear with him in glory."

The play we watch is such a little part of real life; it ends and we go on. Our life now is such a little part of real life, and when it ends, if we know him, we go on with him. The coming of Christ for us may be like our leaving the theater; whether we wept or laughed, we're ready to get on with living.

 Lord, help me to see Christ's coming not as an ending but a beginning.

What can I do today to be better prepared for his coming?

■ WAITING FOR THE DAWN

Isa. 21:11-12: "Watchman, what is left of the night? The watchman replies, 'Morning is coming.'"

It was early one night when I was called to the telephone to learn the news—my dad had died. I was on a trip away from home. I went back to my hotel room and began to pack. Friends helped make arrangements for a flight later that night. After packing, all that was left for me to do was to wait and think and remember. A friend came, talked with me a little, hugged me while I wept, listened as I told him a little about my dad, and prayed.

Then came that late-night flight. I sat by the window watching for the first streaks of dawn. I didn't want night anymore; I wanted dawn.

The watchmen of ancient Israel hoped for dawn and looked for it, scanning the sky. A late-night traveler, heavy with sorrow, watches for the dawn too.

Hope came to the world at dawn on resurrection morning. Jesus was alive! I thought of that as I watched the sky. And then I saw them—the first streaks of dawn. The sun's rays, like the promise of hope, became brighter and brighter and brighter.

 Thank you, Lord, that hope, like the dawning light, fills every corner of my life.

Plan a morning when you can watch a sunrise and focus on the hope and love of God.

■ ALONE

Ps. 102:1-7:   "I am like a desert owl, like an owl among the ruins" (v. 6).

It is so difficult to be alone—not the alone of a quiet room at the end of a day when you don't really want to talk to anyone, but the lonely feeling in a crowd, at a party when conversations are shallow and no one is really close.

Sometimes we, too, feel as the psalmist felt. We are like an owl in the desert, totally out of place and alone.

Jesus knew what it was to be alone. We think it was always pleasant for him because of the nearness of his heavenly Father, but Jesus, too, was alone sometimes like you and me.

We can be glad for the goodness of God, glad for his nearness, but still not be able to laugh with others, except lightly. God understands, and perhaps knowing what all of us would face from time to time, he had a special purpose in allowing the psalmist to write those words about the owl. Maybe this is one of those passages that Paul was referring to when he said, "For whatsoever things were written aforetime were written for our learning, that we through patience and comfort of the scriptures might have hope" (Rom. 15:4 KJV).

Lord, in my lonely times I thank you that I'm not apart from you.

Today call someone who might be alone. He or she may need you, especially now.

16

■ STANDING ON HOLY GROUND

Exod. 3:4-5: "When the Lord saw that he had gone over to look, God called to him from within the bush, 'Moses, Moses!' And Moses said, 'Here I am.' 'Do not come any closer,' God said. 'Take off your sandals, for the place where you are standing is holy ground.' "

Moses didn't know that he was standing on holy ground; God had to tell him. We hope for special times of worship, warm relationships with God, and sometimes we're disappointed. We want something more, even shopping for it in different churches. Yet often we're on holy ground already, and we don't even know it. Like Moses, we don't recognize where we are or Who is there with us.

God is near. We can approach him. And when we gather with other believers, we're assured, "Where two or three are gathered together in my name, there am I in the midst of them" (Matt. 18:20 KJV).

Sometimes, because we confuse entertainment with worship, an emotional high with the presence of God, a dramatic event with the still small voice, we go looking for the unusual, the extraordinary, the spectacular. God often meets us in the simple. Then God has to tell us what we should have discovered ourselves: that we're on holy ground.

Lord, help me to recognize you wherever I am.

Determine to go to church or approach your quiet time with God expectantly. Don't look for a dramatic event to tell you that you are on holy ground.

■ GOOD ADVICE

Ps. 34:1-8: "Taste and see that the Lord is good; blessed is the man who takes refuge in him" (v. 8).

Have you done that? Have you tried what David is asking you to do? Have you tasted so that you'll see that the Lord is good? That's not a casual request; that's a serious challenge. For once you taste, you won't go elsewhere for satisfaction.

Sometimes people who are without hope—sad, depressed people—need only a little taste. When I'm sick and I don't want to eat, I recall words I heard when I was a little boy: "Taste it," I was told, as a spoonful of broth was put to my lips. There is something about tasting, getting the flavor, that makes the juices start flowing, and then we want more. And as we take more, our strength comes back. "Taste," we are told. Perhaps that means taking hold of a portion of Scripture, singing a snatch of a hymn, reciting a recalled children's prayer—just taste. See? You will discover that he is good.

When you're too depressed or too weak from life's conflicts to feast on the Lord, then take David's counsel: "Taste." You'll see.

 When I don't feel ready for your banquet table, help me, Lord, to take David's advice to taste and see.

Today, memorize a promise of Scripture that may not seem to have anything in it that pertains to the way you feel right now. On the days that are not so good it will come back to you and help you.

IS THIS A GOOD ONE?

Matt. 13:27-30:   "Let both grow together until the harvest" (v. 30).

When I was a little boy, our family had a garden. On Saturdays when my dad went out to weed the garden, my brother and I went along to "help," although I suppose we didn't do much more than get in dad's way. I couldn't tell weeds from good plants and can remember calling out, "Is this a good one, dad?" And he would tell me—again—"This is a good one; that's a weed." Dad always knew the difference.

God knows the difference too. God planted good seed, but the garden isn't free of weeds. Jesus taught that the bad seed doesn't just drop in by itself. "An enemy comes and sows it," he said. But at the risk of tearing out something worthwhile, weeds are left until harvest.

Harvest time is coming. Then the good fruit will be gathered into God's barns, the weeds gathered for the fire.

I still can't always tell good plants from bad. Too often they look alike to my untrained eye. But God knows. And someday, at the gathering in, if we should ask, "Is this a good one?" God will know.

 Thank you, Lord, that I don't have to judge people. You are the judge; you know the good plants from the weeds.

If you know someone who thinks the wicked prosper as much or more than the righteous, tell that person about God's garden.

HOPE BRINGS DESIRES FOR PURITY

1 John 3:1-3: "Everyone who has this hope in him purifies himself, just as he is pure" (v. 3).

Take away hope from a person, and the person won't care anymore. Give someone hope, and he tries harder. With hope we build; without hope we give up. Hope says, "Go for it." Lack of hope says, "Why bother?"

Hope and purity go together. When someone has hope, that person also wants to be pure. Why? Not because the individual is afraid to try new things that might be corrupting, but because the person has hope, has tomorrow, has a reason for being pure—both for now and for eternity. Hope says, "This isn't all there is." Hope gives a high view of now, because it gives a high view of where life is leading. With that high view of hope comes purity. Are you living for purity? If you have hope in Christ, you are.

Hope and impurity are contradictions. But when we have hope, we want purity, because when we are in Christ we have a future. We want to stay pure for ourselves, for our loved ones, and for God.

Lord, because I have hope in my life, may I live a pure life.

Purposely and prayerfully, commit to God one impure area in your life with the sincere prayer that God take it away.

■ ALL NIGHT ALONE

Luke 6:12-16: "One of those days Jesus went out into the hills to pray, and spent the night praying to God" (v. 12).

We've all done that, not always because we had a major decision to make, as Jesus did, but sometimes we've been up all night in prayer because of troubles. Pain is all around us. People suffer some horrible agonies. A runaway daughter, a drug-addicted son, a cancer-riddled spouse, an emotional struggle. So we pray. Sometimes we pray all night.

Those all-night times of praying come to all of us, and when they do, we don't want people coming around later giving us pat answers or clichés. We don't need guilt added to our suffering with statements such as, "Well, if you only had enough faith," or "have you confessed all your sins?" We want understanding.

When he made the choice of who his disciples would be, Jesus was alone. He was alone again when he agonized in the garden before he went to the cross. He went through nights of prayer long before we did. He is our example of trust. And because he is, he is also our example of hope.

 Lord, help me to recognize that Jesus knows what I'm going through. He had his all-night prayer times too.

Be alert to someone around you who may be going through a painful time. Help him, knowing that he may be going through some difficult nights alone.

■ A WALL OF PEACE

Phil. 4:6-9: "And the peace of God, which transcends all understanding, will guard your hearts and your minds in Christ Jesus" (v. 7).

Night doesn't always end with a bright sunrise. Sometimes morning comes with a gray and cloudy sky.

There are times when we live in a gray world, not because God made it so but because sin blocks the light. There is sin all around us, and it erodes, corrupts, destroys. Our world is like that. We are told that all of creation has been groaning, waiting for redemption (Rom. 8:22-23).

But God is here, too, even when we don't see all of his beauty and light. Just as God's peace surrounds us on dark nights, it is a wall, a fence, a protection on the gray days, too, and we are safe. While we grope through the day, we still have hope for better times, because we still have God, even when the light is temporarily blocked.

God's peace is a protection. But it isn't just what we grasp or understand about peace that protects. His protection goes beyond our understanding. God's peace guards the heart and the mind in Christ Jesus all the time, during the dark nights and the gray days.

 Thank you, Lord, that I don't have to have sunshine and reassurance constantly to know that your peace is a protective wall around me.

Envision that wall of God's peace surrounding you today and take comfort in it.

■ CELEBRATION

1 Thess. 4:13-18: "Brothers, we do not want you to be ignorant about those who fall asleep, or to grieve like the rest of men, who have no hope" (v. 13).

There are tears at funeral services. At some funerals we cry because we're going to miss the one who's gone for a little while until that day when we'll be together again for all eternity. But at other funerals we cry because we know that the one gone had no hope of eternity; he would not transfer faith from himself to Jesus Christ. For those we sorrow because there is no hope. Peter said: "Salvation is found in no one else, for there is no other name under heaven given to men by which we must be saved" (Acts 4:12).

But how much joy there is at the funeral of a believer when we rejoice at what is already being experienced by that loved one who is with the Lord. Then death is a celebration, a coronation, a commencement.

Those who have no hope cry because life has ended. Existence on this earth was all there was. But for one who belonged to Jesus there are tears, yes, but sorrow? No. Do we sorrow when an award is given? Do we sorrow when a prize is won? Do we sorrow when health is regained, when there is no more pain, when a person isn't tired anymore?

 Thank you, Lord, for the assurance that in Christ we have hope in death. Help us to offer comfort to others based on your Word.

Write a note today to someone you know who has recently lost a loved one. Give that person God's promise.

■ EQUAL ACCESS

Rom. 5:1-5: "Through whom we have gained access by faith into this grace in which we now stand. And we rejoice in the hope of the glory of God" (v. 2).

We read a lot about equal-access laws. In Christ we have equal access, for he is our access. He is the door, an entryway. Noting how shepherds often physically lay across the opening of a sheepfold at night to keep the sheep in and predators out, Jesus said, "I am the gate" (John 10:9).

But what if we choose to ignore him and seek our own way, the way that Jesus said was the way of the thieves and robbers? Then we miss out on his offer. Jesus is our access. In him we can rejoice in hope, we can glory in tribulation, for we have peace with God. We have walked through the doorway into God's grace, his favor.

But if when we have access by faith before us, we refuse to step through by faith, we are saying "no" to grace. Then we have no ground upon which to stand. We cannot rejoice. There is no hope. Tribulation overwhelms.

We can stand in God's unmerited favor and rejoice in hope if by faith we have walked through the door. Have you done that?

 Lord Jesus, help me to walk through this wide open door to hope and glory. And help me to see that the step is taken by faith.

If you know someone who is stumbling at the idea of believing by faith, help him to see that it is like walking through a door. Then, invite him to walk through.

2 Cor. 5:1-6: "Now we know that if the earthly tent we live in is destroyed, we have a building from God, an eternal house in heaven, not built by human hands" (v. 1).

*H*ow we will die is yet unknown to most of us; *that* we will die is certain. If God should take you home suddenly, without opportunity to let others experience your dying, that is God's right. But if God allows you to die more slowly, then know also that God will give you many chances to let others learn from you how to die. They will watch, they will observe your emotions, and they will see the evidence of your faith. Your greatest witness may come in your last moments on this earth.

The thief on the cross learned how to die at the last minute, but what a profound impact his death has had on the world.

I've read the book *The Man Who Lived Twice,* the story of actor Edward Sheldon. He knew how to die and helped others while he was doing it. He gave to others for as long as he had life.

How we live is critical; how we die is critical too.

 O God, show me how to use my last moments of life for your glory and as a witness to others who still may be uncertain about salvation and faith.

Take a moment in the days ahead to write down the way you would like to live your remaining years and who you would like to influence if God gives you that opportunity.

■ "WHAT WILL IT BE?"

Titus 3:5-7: "So that, having been justified by his grace, we might become heirs having the hope of eternal life" (v. 7).

What will it be to be there?" asked the Scots Presbyterian preacher, Alexander White, who served as pastor of Free St. George's, Edinburgh, for 40 years. Then this 19th-century preacher with disturbing words would add, "And what will it be not to be there?"

Heaven awaits those justified by God's grace. To all who place their trust in Jesus Christ is promised a position as heirs according to the hope of eternal life. But what awaits those who say no?

"I'll party with my friends," say some who have no heavenly hope. But they won't, for outer darkness is separation, not only from God but from everyone else.

What will it be like to be there? Reunion with friends and loved ones. The joy of God's glorious presence. No pain, no sorrow. Living forever and ever in light and happiness. What will it be like not to be there? What will it be like to be alone and in darkness and separated from the One who is light and life?

Disturbing words, "What will it be not to be there?" are balanced by awesome and wonderful words, "What will it be to be there?"

Dear God, I thank you that through faith in Christ I know, on the assurance of his Word, that I have eternal life and that I'll "be there."

Have you spoken to anyone about heaven recently? Would you speak to someone about heaven today?

■ TRUST AND WAIT

Ps. 130:1-8: "I wait for the Lord, my soul waits, and in his word I put my hope" (v. 5).

Stillness filled the cabin of the inbound 747. We were enroute from Seoul, Korea, to Hong Kong. Over Okinawa two tropical storms that had been in divergent paths began to merge. Air traffic had been suspended from Okinawa hours before when tropical storm Holly hit. Now with back winds extending 400 nautical miles out to sea, Holly's perimeter was joined by the sudden shift of tropical storm Gerald moving northward. We were in the middle of the pincer. The captain warned us that the last miles would be the roughest. No one was reading, no one was sleeping, no one was talking. There was silence in the cabin as we anticipated the slam of the jumbo jet into the high winds of the storms.

And we waited. Each minute passing was almost an announcement in itself. We were that much closer to land. Rain sleeted against the plane windows. Lightning cut across and around us. But we missed both storms and rode in without a quiver.

Our lives are often like that plane ride. We wait, we anticipate, and we hope. The psalmist knew it. Sometimes the storm hits, sometimes it doesn't. Our task: trust and wait.

 Thank you, Lord, that when the storms threaten me I can wait and trust and in your Word put my hope.

If high winds of adversity are buffeting your life, remember your waiting is not by days or by hours but a minute at a time. Each minute, you get closer to making it through.

■ MERCY IN THE DARK TIMES

Ps. 33:18-22: "May your unfailing love rest upon us, O Lord, even as we put our hope in you" (v. 22).

We err when we paint a glorious picture of the Christian life being nothing more than the "good life" in social, political or economic terms. It is the good life, because it is God-given life, and God *is* good. But that doesn't mean what the easy-answer people say it means. The disciples, faithful in following Jesus, had hard times. Down through the centuries the martyrs have had hard times. In many parts of the world Christians live out their commitment based not on ease but on an obedience and a desire to follow Christ in spite of persecution.

When we recognize that life is not easy, we too are more likely to ask, "May your unfailing love rest upon us, O Lord, even as we put our hope in you." God gives merciful love. When we call, there comes the intervention of God in our affairs.

Though there may be suffering, God gives hope to hold to. In the dark times, the painful times, the times when all seems humanly hopeless, we still have God. God's mercy is our hope.

Lord, I know that your mercy is there. Help me to hope in your mercy.

Through your denomination or mission-sending board, write a letter today to Christians in another part of the world who may need encouragement and hope. Tell them that though you have not met, you are praying for them today.

■ PUSHING OR WAITING?

Lam. 3:22-26: "I say to myself, 'The Lord is my portion; therefore I will wait for him'" (v. 24).

Open your mail today, and you'll probably find at least one request to sign a petition, to get behind this cause or that one, to object, picket, declare your stand, join a power bloc or political party, make people see things "our way." This is not so different from what the medieval Crusaders did, except we don't carry swords.

Is our hope based on being right and forcing others to admit it? Or is our hope as it was for Jeremiah, that the Lord is our portion, that our hope is in him, that we seek him and quietly wait for the salvation of the Lord.

Of course we must stand against evil of all kinds. The Scriptures are not silent, nor must we be, about the evil around us. But we lose our true hope, our biblical perspective, even our trust in God, when we sell out to programs on how to make things happen our way. Though we are to be as wise as serpents, we are not power seekers or power brokers. We can never be manipulators or hateful egotists. "The Lord is good to those whose hope is in him. It is good to wait quietly for the salvation of the Lord" (vv. 25-26).

Quiet waiting is much more biblical than violent pushing.

 Lord, once I have taken a position on evil as best I know how, help me to wait patiently for your help.

Today take a spiritual inventory of the three or four social issues that you feel require your stand. Commit them to God.

■ BEING SURE

Heb. 11:1-40: "And without faith it is impossible to please God, because anyone who comes to him must believe that he exists and that he rewards those who earnestly seek him" (v. 6).

Maybe in your reflective moments you're thinking, "I had hope once." Then you begin to think, "Maybe it wasn't hope; maybe it was youthful optimism." "I was going to go to college." "I was going to marry Jim." "I was going to have a brilliant career." Those were dreams, aspirations. It was all going to be so good. You had such hope.

Maybe you had spiritual hope too. "God can do anything. God can do far more than I could ask or think." What happened? Did I ask amiss, to spend it on my own pleasures, as James stated? Did I have hope but not faith?

The ancients were commended for being sure. Without faith it is impossible to please God. Maybe I have been trying to claim the second part of the promise without fully accepting the first, because anyone who comes to God must believe (1) that God exists and (2) that God rewards those who earnestly seek him. God exists to be God, not just to reward me. Do I glorify him or do I try to use him? Regardless of my past behavior, what am I doing now?

O God, help me to have faith as the patriarchs did.

Make a list of what you "hope for" now and ask yourself, "Is this based on my earnestly seeking God?" You will learn what items to keep on your list and which ones to cross out.

■ SEEING AGAIN

Matt. 20:29-34: " 'Lord,' they answered, 'we want our sight' " (v. 33).

Two blind men sat by the roadside in Jericho. There is an oasis there, a good spring and shade trees. Jesus was coming, and they waited in the shade. They had hope. When he came near, they called, "Jesus, Son of David, have mercy on us!"

The story is short. Jesus healed them; he gave them their sight. Their hope was fulfilled.

But I have my spiritual eyesight, you say. Is there a story of hope for me here? Look again. It isn't in the English translation but it is in the Greek: "They saw again." Again! They had not been born blind. Once they had seen. They had known beauty, the sunlight, a child's smile, a loved one's look. They had seen it, but now all was dark. Still, Jesus was coming by. Their hope was coming.

Have you known sight, real sight? You know what it is to have been in God's sunlight enjoying his smile. Have you given up hope of ever having that again? Those blind men hadn't, and Jesus touched them. They saw again.

No matter how long your sight has been fading or how long you've sat by the side of life's spiritual road, Jesus will touch you if you'll call on him. You'll see again. That's hope!

Lord Jesus, give me clear spiritual eyesight again.

What spiritual touch do you need? Have you asked for it?

■ BACK TO BASICS

1 Cor. 13:8-13: "And now these three remain: faith, hope and love. But the greatest of these is love" (v. 13).

Hope never stands alone. It is part of faith, and it goes with love. All three are centered in God. You can have faith, and you can have love. But they do not stand apart from hope.

We come to real hope the same way we come to real faith and real love, when we come back to our basic need, which is God himself. That's when peripheral things are pushed aside—perhaps at a funeral, at the loss of a job, in a hospital bed. It isn't a matter of grasping at straws or hoping against hope. Quite the opposite, it's a coming back to what only God can give. A mother whose baby is struggling for breath isn't thinking about her hair appointment. A young man with his legs pinned under a wrecked car isn't thinking about missing the start of a movie. When life becomes more real, so does hope.

Hope, like love and faith, goes deep. Some reject the necessity of hope and try to skip along through life on the surface until eventually they break through. When they do, they either drown in despair or turn to grab for the hope they've so long pretended didn't matter. When we get to the basics, only three things matter—faith in God, the love of God, and hope given by God.

 Lord, may I be basic in my understanding of hope. May it be as clear to my thinking as faith and love.

Begin a daily program of searching the Scriptures, underlining those words that speak to you of hope.

◼ HOPE SO LARGE

1 Peter 1:3-5: "In his great mercy he has given us new birth into a living hope through the resurrection of Jesus Christ from the dead" (v. 3).

What do you look forward to? What do you daydream about concerning tomorrow? A holiday trip? A hike in the mountains? Fishing on a northern lake? Is it thinking about the next salary increase and what you're going to do with it? Is it the addition you are going to put on your house, perhaps next year? Is it the job applications after graduation? Your wedding?

Is hope only those things? Or is it bigger? Peter praised God, who has given us a living hope, the resurrection of Jesus Christ from the dead, and has brought us into an inheritance that cannot perish, spoil, or fade. It is a kept inheritance—guarded or locked up in heaven—for you.

Look at your life. Can you say that what you hope for is something that will neither perish, spoil, nor fade? In ourselves hope is tiny. In God hope is large. In ourselves we grasp so little of hope, but when we see God and offer praise, we begin to move from the little, the fading, the spoiling, the perishing, to the great, the untarnished, the unspoiled, and the unfading. Whatever hopes you have today, let them be centered in the big hope—Jesus Christ.

 Lord, may I move past the corruptible, the decaying, my temporary hopes, and see what really counts—hope centered in you.

Take a trip to the junkyard and realize that everything that is there was once craved as important by someone. Then the next time your hope goes from the great to the tiny, think about the junkyard.

■ DON'T MISS THE TEACHING

Acts 1:6-9: "It is not for you to know the times or dates the Father has set by his own authority" (v. 7).

Years ago I met a tour leader who takes people to the Holy Land to "see how prophecy has been fulfilled." I found myself thinking, "If the prophecy has been fulfilled, people don't need to go see it." If they find fulfillment in the land being Israel, the fact that it is blooming and flowing more with milk and honey than ever before and is militarily strong, that's interesting. But the value of a tour is in understanding Scripture better by understanding the land in which God's revelation took place.

Our hope is not built on what we determine is happening, has happened, or will happen, but on God who makes it all happen, and who God is as the totally omnipotent, holy One. Even if we see nothing of prophetic fulfillment in Israel or elsewhere, he is still God. God's power, his Godhead, is not measured by how much prophecy we see fulfilled or not fulfilled. Jesus told us that we are not to know the times and dates. God alone has that knowledge. Wouldn't it be sad if we were so busy looking at times and dates that we missed the whole teaching of the One who said not to do it.

Lord, as I live my life, let me be content that you know what I do not need to know.

Start each day with the thought, "I won't look for signs so much as I will look for him." Live with anticipation that Christ could come before the sun goes down today.

■ ANTICIPATION

Titus 2:11-14: "While we wait for the blessed hope—the glorious appearing of our great God and Savior, Jesus Christ" (v. 13).

In his book *The Return of the Lord Jesus*, Reuben A. Torrey said, "The coming again of Jesus Christ is the one doctrine with which God commands us to comfort sorrowing saints" (See 1 Thess. 4:18).

The Lord's coming is our blessed hope, and it is with that hope that we can comfort the sorrowing. His coming is not just a hope for our dying, making possible our going to heaven to be with him, although that is a precious promise. But in the promise of his appearing, we have a sure hope that Christ will not forget those who belong to him. For Jesus promised: "Whoever comes to me I will never drive away" (John 6:37).

But the coming again of Jesus is also a warning. There are people who are still trusting in themselves. What a tragedy that is, for the greatest idol is a self-idol, and no idol can give hope.

Jesus made a point of saying that he was coming back because he wanted us to know that. We can depend on it and comfort others with the promise of it. And, because we are depending on it, we are able to say no to ungodliness. Instead, we can lead controlled, obedient lives, awaiting that glorious hope.

 Lord, thank you for the promise of Jesus' glorious appearing. Help me to live in anticipation of that.

With whom can I share my anticipation today? Who needs the comfort that comforts me?

■ ANSWER

1 Peter 3:15-16: "Always be prepared to give an answer to everyone who asks you to give the reason for the hope that you have (v. 15).

It can happen any time. I was sitting with other journalists at a press-club luncheon when one man began talking more and more vociferously about "reality vs. religion." He was angry about those people who believe in God and thus "do not face reality." I didn't argue with him, but I did ask him some questions, particularly, "What do you mean by reality?"

We never know when we're going to be called upon to give a reason for the hope that we have. And many times we have no evidence that a person accepts what we say. But our responsibility is to be faithful, to drop seeds of truth where we can, taking whatever opportunity is at hand to tell why we have committed our lives to Jesus Christ.

That luncheon ended in a stalemate. Yet maybe that man went home thinking about some statement that I made.

We live in trust that God will turn to profit a faithful word. We don't have to win arguments; we do have to be prepared to give an answer.

 Lord, help me to spend enough time in your Word and with you in prayer to be ready at any time to give your truth to someone.

Bible memorization is one of the best ways to be prepared to give an answer about your faith. Have you started on a Bible memory plan?

■ TURNING AWAY, TURNING BACK

Jer. 17:13-17: "All who forsake you will be put to shame. Those who turn away from you will be written in the dust" (v. 13).

Some of the greatest tragedies in this world are not what happens to people but what people do to themselves. There is something terribly sad about a person who drifts from an early conviction and trust in God to a worship of wealth and pleasure. House payments take the tithe, networking and social commitments cut into worship, drink and sometimes drugs become the preferred choice for seeking joy and peace—two descriptions of the spiritual fruit of God.

David learned what straying meant and prayed, "Create in me a pure heart, O God, and renew a steadfast spirit within me" (Ps. 51:10). God honored that prayer and called David "a man after my own heart" (Acts 13:22). But another king, Asa, who also once walked with God, would not come back—and grew angry at the suggestion that he should. When he died, he got a fancy funeral, but there was never any mention that he came back to the faith of his youth.

No one has to forsake faith. That's a choice each of us makes. We don't have to be put to shame. Drifting can happen to any of us. But our hope knows that we can return as David did.

 Lord, if sin takes hold of me, please keep me from allowing any idols to block my turning back to you.

Think about what may have become more important to you than God. Will you confess it now and turn back to God?

■ BUILDING WELL

Matt. 23:37-39: "Look, your house is left to you" (v. 38).

In this one brief sentence is a profound indictment, an awful emphasis: "Your house is left to you." Some translations add the word "desolate," but that word is missing in the Greek.

The day will come when all some people will have is what they've built with their own hands. We're told that "Unless the Lord builds the house, its builders labor in vain" (Ps. 127:1). Some spend their lifetime in building. What they build is all they have, and at the end there is no gift, no reward, no crown.

You say, "But I've built well. Look how well I've done." In the light of eternity, how long will what you have built last? The disciples pointed out to Jesus the beauty of the temple. Had anything ever elicited such awe? Jesus said, "You don't even know that not one stone will be left upon another," and it wasn't. In less than 70 years it was all gone, just ruins.

What are you building your hope on? What is this structure of your life that you are hammering together with your own strength? Will you come to the end and have only that? Or will you place your hope in God?

෴ Dear Lord, be the master builder of my life.

Look around your physical house which you labored so hard to build. Look at its foundation, the cracks, the sand holes in the cement, the places where water is already coming in. Be sure your life is not like that.

Ps. 146:5-10: "Blessed is he whose help is the God of Jacob, whose hope is in the Lord his God" (v. 5).

If you have ever been a surgical patient, you know that there were some people on your floor who rested easily the night before surgery and others who were miserable. You know how you felt too. Doctors and nurses have long known that people of faith, those who have hope, are much more at ease about surgery than those who do not have a vital, living relationship with God. People without hope clutch and cling to life. People with hope can relax in the certainty that God has them. And, as a result, after surgery the trusting ones usually heal better and even faster.

People of hope have a resource. People without hope do not. All they've ever trusted in has been themselves, and in surgery they don't have control anymore. Though most people may succeed in trusting the surgeon, the believer trusts God who has the believer in his hand and therefore the surgeon in his hand as well.

There are 95 references to hope in the Old Testament and 85 references in the New Testament. Surely God placed those references there for all seasons and occasions of life.

 Thank you, Lord, for hope, and your promise that goes with me even to a hospital surgical ward.

Is there someone you know facing surgery or who is facing some struggle who needs a visit from you today? Will you be a hope bringer?

■ IN SPITE OF CIRCUMSTANCES

Ps. 119:73-76: "May they who fear you rejoice when they see me, for I have put my hope in your word" (v. 74).

Many people know where hope comes from but they don't know how to get it, how to have it, and how not to lose it.

When a Christian dentist lost one of his arms in an accident, he struggled with the realization, "It is never going to be any different." Whatever is troubling you—finances, health, parents, children—maybe it is never going to be any different—or, at least, not be different for a long time. Maybe, like that amputee trying to practice dentistry, that's the way it is.

But it's in those situations that we place our trust and hope in God. And when others see it, they are encouraged to trust too. They know that, like the dentist, we cannot grow another arm. We have to live with what is. That doesn't negate the power of God or prayer. It doesn't mean that God can't change things or perform miracles. He can.

The one who can say, "Your hands made me. Give me understanding," is the one who can also say, "May they who fear you rejoice when they see me." Why? Because in spite of my circumstances, I can put my hope in God.

Dear God, life is not always fair. But I thank you that I have hope in you. May others see it.

Think about that major troubling problem in your life. Instead of fighting against it, yield it to God.

■ EXCITEMENT

Rom. 12:9-16: "Be joyful in hope, patient in affliction, faithful in prayer" (v. 12).

The visiting author promised to give away a free copy of his newest book. I found myself with rising hope that the recipient would be me, becoming more excited as the time for the announcement grew closer. But I didn't get the book; someone else did.

Watch a child when he knows he's going to receive birthday presents, or watch a dog when his master says, "Bone?" Their bodies quiver with excitement.

What excites you? What is your book or toy or bone? Is it a dividend check? Your education completed? Election to an office? A new purchase? An approaching wedding?

God's hope produces joy. Scripture tells us that affliction calls for patience. But hope—that is, the hope we have in Christ, his redeeming hope, the hope of his return—is something to get excited about. We may be faithful in hope, even patient in hope. But as we are when anticipating any good thing, we can also quiver with hope. Joy fills with hope and hope fills with joy, just as Scripture said it would.

Lord, fill me with the joy of my blessed hope in you.

As you read the sought-after book, become bored with the toys, and consume the bones, learn to distinguish between those things and real hope. Then consciously let hope begin to be the joy filler of your life.

TAKE HOPE

Ps. 31:22-24: "Be strong and take heart, all you who hope in the Lord" (v. 24).

In our mixed-up world we still believe in a Creator who had a plan when he made the world and each one of us. If our being were some fluke in a cosmic roll of the dice, there would be no distinction in our personalities, no reason for being what we were created to be. But God affirms our creation, our unique and distinct place in his world. God's special touch brought us into being.

We have hope because we believe in Jesus Christ who left the glory he had with the Father, became one with us, died on the cross, and rose again for our redemption. And, though the world as a whole may still be saying no, we have hope, even in a world like this. We take the counsel of the psalmist, "Be strong and take heart, all you who hope in the Lord." With our eyes wide open to the world around us, we take our hope in the Lord.

Dear God, I'm not blind. I see what the world is. But I also know what you intended in creation, in redemption. I take my hope in you.

As you read your newspaper today, take a felt-tipped pen and next to the stories of corruption and crime and hurt and war write again and again the words, "Be strong and take heart, all you who hope in the Lord." It will change your perspective and you'll never forget that verse.

◼ IT'S NOT TOO LATE

Matt. 20:1-16: "You also go and work in my vineyard" (v. 7).

At first glance it doesn't seem fair. Those who worked all day received the same wages as those who worked only one hour. But take a second look. Those who worked all day contracted for a certain number of hours for a certain amount of pay. They got exactly what they agreed to, and they had the privilege of doing meaningful work. But there were others who had to stand by as first one group and then another was selected. They waited while the day was disappearing. Would there be no work for them, no wage to take home, no money to buy that day's food? Would they return home dragging their feet, head bowed, convinced, "Nobody wants me" or "I have nothing to offer"?

But right at the end, the landowner came around again, and some were hired at five o'clock. Some probably went home before then saying, "It's useless. There's no hope. There's only an hour's work time left." But had they stayed and waited and hoped, they would have been hired.

Jesus told that parable for a reason. Some of us may not be the first given meaningful work in God's vineyard, or even be the midday people. Some of us may be five o'clock people. But we need not give up hope.

 Thank you, Lord, that no matter what time it is in my life, you offer hope for meaningful work.

Do you know someone who feels life has passed him by? Give him this parable; give him this hope.

■ FOR ME

Ps. 22:9-11: "From birth I was cast upon you" (v. 10).

From the moment of birth, in fact from the moment of conception, we are what we are by the blessing of God. When we get hold of that thought, we can begin to see the hand of God leading step by step in our lives, not only from birth but even before that, in the bringing together of great-grandparents and grandparents and parents to produce this unique individual referred to as "me."

Then when we look at God's guidance in placing us where he did, giving what he has given—the friends, the acquaintances, the culture—we see that God has looked after everything. And when we take the promises of Scripture and realize that they're personal, we are able to say, "The redemption freely offered in Jesus Christ, is for me. He went to the cross for me. He rose for me."

When I read John 3:16, the "whoever" in that verse is me. Scriptures take on new meaning when I understand that "All Scripture is given by inspiration of God, and is profitable" for me (2 Tim. 3:16 KJV). And I realize that someday he's coming again for me. Then I can see history for me, the present for me and the future for me. I can say with the psalmist, "From birth I was cast upon you."

Loving God, let me take nothing for granted. I thank you for your creative and saving power.

Ask your parents and grandparents to either write out or talk into a cassette tape their memories of God's leading in their lives. It will encourage and refresh you and show you your spiritual heritage.

■ FIGHTING THE WAVES

Rom. 8:24-27: "Who hopes for what he already has?" (v. 24).

Little boys like to go fishing with their dads. When I was a boy, I did too. One day in the middle of a lake we faced a danger I'll never forget. My brother and I were in a rented boat with dad. He couldn't afford the motor rental, so dad rowed—out into the middle of the lake, which was big, even measured by adult eyes.

Suddenly a storm came up, with the wind blowing off shore. Dad pulled up anchor and started to row, but he couldn't fight the waves which were building higher and higher. My brother and I, frightened, bailed water as dad kept rowing, bending his back against the waves that seemed to want to push us further out into the deep.

We had a lot of hope that day, and we made it to shore. But when we reached land, we didn't have to hope anymore. The apostle Paul said it's always that way. We hope for what we do not have.

We have not arrived yet at the eternal shore. We're not at home and safe yet. And so we hope and battle the waves. We can see the shore; we want to reach it. We bend our backs, and we hope. Then when we arrive, we don't have to hope anymore.

 Dear God, I thank you for the blessed hope that gives certainty of salvation now in Christ and salvation in all of its fullness when we arrive at last on shore.

You may know people who are going through tough times right now. Make sure that they are certain of their security in Christ. Then help them row against the waves.

RACHEL'S CHILDREN

Jer. 31:15-17: " 'They will return from the land of the enemy. So there is hope for your future, declares the Lord" (vv. 16-17).

Jeremiah was talking about Rachel, but he could have been describing mothers today. So many weep for their children, not because they have been captured by some outside force, or enslaved by an invading enemy, or lost because of war or politics or economics. Mothers are weeping because their children are enslaved by a different kind of captivity, a new form of slavery, self-imposed. And mothers wonder as they cry, "Will they return from the land of the enemy? Will God's promise be true for my son or daughter? Will they return?"

There is a promise given: "There is hope for your future. . . . Your children will return." If you and I did not have that same promise, how could we endure? There's not a family or a church congregation that doesn't know the heartache of captured, enslaved children who are gone.

Yet are they forever gone? " 'There is hope for your future,' declares the Lord." And there is.

 Thank you, Lord, for children who are safe within the boundaries. I pray for those today who are not.

You know a hurting family whose children have gone off into their own self-made slavery. Pray for that family today. Comfort them. And if you are that "Rachel," seek the comfort of someone who will pray with you.

■ THE ONLY REAL REFUGE

Joel 3:14-16: "But the Lord will be a refuge for his people" (v. 16).

One of the hardest lessons we learn in life is that neither a person, nor a position, nor a title, nor a fortune can be to us what God alone can be. When troubles come and we are in our valley of decision, we're there alone with God.

Young adults, newly married, think that their spouse will be everything that they need. But no one can be to us what God alone can be. Older people facing life's struggles look to people to help, and some can, but no one can do what God alone can do. Business people look to what they have accumulated and the power they wield. It doesn't help.

We need accomplishments, a measure of success, adequate funds, a meaningful vocation, but there is no permanent refuge in any of those.

We need good strong relationships. People encourage us, support us, help us, love us. We're happy when we have friends and family nearby. But people are people, with all their own frailties and weaknesses. God is God, with neither frailty nor weakness. The wise person has discovered that.

Lord, keep me from expecting of people and things what I can only expect of you.

Be a friend to someone today who is going through a dark night or a valley of decision. But don't pretend to have all the answers for that person. Just be there to pray and support.

■ A DAY AT A TIME

Job 7:6-9: "My days are swifter than a weaver's shuttle, and they come to an end without hope" (v. 6).

Job was depressed, and he had a right to be. With the loss of his family, the loss of his wealth, and then the loss of his health, he was a shattered man. Maybe God encouraged the story about Job to be written in order to tell us about such things as pain and despair and the feelings of hopelessness. Now, because this book is in the Bible, we have something that Job didn't have; we know the outcome of Job's story. He had to live a day at a time without ever having some other previous Job to look to. We have Job's story; we know how God healed and blessed and brought him into good days again.

There are needed lessons here because the struggles and brevity of our life is so real to us. We waken in the morning having no idea what a day will bring. Suddenly there is a telephone call, a news bulletin, a pathology report, and all is changed.

Our days are swift, swifter than a weaver's shuttle, and though there are times, as was true for Job, when we're convinced that we've come to an end without hope, we learn as Job learned that that's not true. We can still cling to God.

 Dear God, help me to be aware of how fast things can happen, but at the same time not to measure the end by what I'm going through now.

Read the entire book of Job, especially the concluding chapters. Hear what God says, see what God does, and take hope.

■ IS YOUR HELMET ON?

1 Thess. 5:5-8: "Putting on faith and love as a breastplate, and the hope of salvation as a helmet" (v. 8).

No soldier goes into battle without a helmet. No construction worker intent on building goes into a work area without his hard hat. No fireman enters a burning building with its falling debris without his fireman's hat. No baseball player steps into the batter's box without his batter's helmet. It's too dangerous. Did you put your helmet on today?

The helmet, Paul says, is the hope of salvation. The hope of salvation has the effect of wearing a helmet. When you have salvation, not as a wispy kerchief but as a firm, hard reality, and you have it on when you face life, then no unexpected explosions, no sudden blows, can topple you.

If hope were nothing but a dream, it wouldn't offer much protection in the battles of life. But hope is firm, it's solid. It protects the part of you that does your thinking. Your mind is guarded by this firm hope of salvation.

We don't just talk about hope; we protect our minds, the central brain of our lives, with the firm reality of our hope in Christ Jesus.

 Thank you, Lord, that when I face the battles of life I not only have the breastplate of love and faith but I have a helmet.

Think of life as a hard-hat area. Think of the hope of salvation as a helmet. It will change your perspective on how you face each day and the events in it.

■ THE BRIDE IS READY

Rev. 19:6-8: "Fine linen, bright and clean, was given her to wear" (v. 8).

We knew them both. They'd been in the Sunday school class my wife and I taught. We'd watched them mature in the faith, meet each other, fall in love, and plan their wedding. The wedding day came. They had talked about it, counted first the months, then the weeks, then the days and hours. Candles were lit, music was played. The bride and groom came together at the altar to exchange their vows before God, and the congregation gathered. There was an excitement about it, a glow on the couple's faces—the joy of anticipation.

John knew something of that. "Rejoice," he said. "Be glad. Give God the glory. For the wedding of the Lamb has come, and the bride is ready." Believers are the bride of Christ. He is coming for his bride, the church, that universal body of committed men and women who have placed their trust in Jesus as Savior and Lord. They prepare their garments; they make ready; they keep themselves pure and clean for him. They're excited; their faces glow. The anticipation is so great. Soon the Lamb will come for his bride; soon the wedding.

Are you anticipating? Is your face aglow? Do you love God?

Lord, help me to be as excited about your coming as that bride and groom were about their marriage.

If Christ should come today or before tomorrow morning, are you prepared? Is all ready? Are you able to face each sunrise with the words, "Perhaps today"?

■ MIRACLES FOLLOW THE PLOW

1 Cor. 9:7-12: "When the plowman plows and the thresher threshes, they ought to do so in the hope of sharing in the harvest" (v. 10).

A. W. Tozer liked to say, "Miracles follow the plow." They do. Jesus said, "No man, having put his hand to the plough, and looking back, is fit for the kingdom of God" (Luke 9:62 KJV). Lot's wife looked back; we know what happened to her. The laborer works in hope, the farmer plows in hope, and that plowing brings miracles—God's miracles. Hope in sharing the harvest is a call to work, a call to keep on looking forward, a call to expect the harvest.

The farmer plowing doesn't see what he hopes for, but it will be there in time. Your faithful plowing may not show you what you hope for, but in time you'll see. When we work for God, we can expect to have a share in the harvest that God will provide when all our plowing and our threshing is done.

Hope is not a dreamy state of gazing at the clouds and wishing for something while the hours drift on. Hope is getting up, getting behind the plow, not looking back, and working as hard as you can. Miracles do follow the plow. That's what hope is all about.

 Thank you, Lord, for the call to hard work and the expectation that goes with it.

Do you tend to give up? What plowing are you doing right now where you can hope for a harvest weeks or months from now?

■ TOO BIG?

2 Cor. 1:8-11: "He has delivered us from such a deadly peril, and he will deliver us. On him we have set our hope that he will continue to deliver us" (v. 10).

I fret and worry that God won't handle a situation that is overwhelming me. I think that because it's too big for me, surely it must be too big for God. Then someone with more objectivity than I have asks the questions that I should have been asking all along: "Remember when you faced a similar impossible situation a few years ago, and how God put all the pieces together?"

"I remember."

"And the time before that when . . ." and he finishes the details that stir the awe that was there when it happened.

"Yes, I remember."

"Well," he continues, "Look at the Scripture."

So I do look, and there it is—Paul's statement about God's deliverance when what was happening to him was much tougher than what is happening to me.

God doesn't want me to be living as if I'm the only hope that I have. If God can raise the dead, what is so impossible about what I am facing now or what you are facing? "He has delivered us, and he will deliver us." With such a promise, and based on his fulfillment before, what is there to doubt?

Thank you, Lord, for the assurance that you have delivered and you will deliver.

Be aware of how often God has intervened in your life and answered your prayers before. Live today knowing that God hasn't quit.

■ KINGDOM

Rev. 11:15-16: "The kingdom of the world has become the kingdom of our Lord and of his Christ, and he will reign for ever and ever" (v. 15).

This Scripture hasn't been completely fulfilled yet, and some people blame God for what is wrong with this world, as if Satan were not prowling and the kingdom had come. The kingdom hasn't come yet, but someday it will come, and Christ will reign forever and ever. That's our hope.

Individually and collectively, the redeemed in Christ look forward to that day. Jesus Christ died for the world, and each of us separately and collectively is a part of that world. Jesus Christ died for all, but specifically he died for you and me. He rose from the grave for all, but specifically for you and me. The world has not all come to the cross; the world has not all acknowledged the resurrection. Only some. But that's enough for the kingdom.

Hope touches the world through you and me and all who love Christ and his appearing. It is our privilege to bring the kingdom message to as many as we can that they too may share in that day when he establishes his rule forever.

 O Lord, help me to be faithful with the message of the kingdom, for so many know nothing of it.

Are you clear in your own mind between Satan's kingdom and God's kingdom? Be sure you know that Christ rules you now and that you will be his when the kingdom comes.

■ OLD AND NEW

2 Peter 3:10-14: "Since everything will be destroyed in this way, what kind of people ought you to be?" (v. 11).

Even the erosion, the changing of what is created, should tell us that we can't put our hope in tangible things. Automobiles rust, houses get old, rocks break down—even the stars burn out. There is nothing in creation that can point to eternal hope.

Eternal hope is based on the One who is outside his creation yet who entered his creation. Our hope is eternal because the source of our hope is eternal. Christians do not believe in some thing; they believe in Someone. That One is God, revealed to us in Christ Jesus.

We don't despair over the ending of all that is. We don't despair about the destruction of the earth, for we are looking forward to something new: a new heaven, a new earth, our new home—the home of the righteous. What we do stand in awe of is the question, "What kind of people ought you to be?" We respond to the biblical answer, "You ought to live holy and godly lives as you look forward to the day of God."

 Lord, help me to put my confidence in you, not things, for even the earth will someday end. Since holiness is what you demand, teach me to be holy.

If this Scripture frightens you, face it. Confronting scary Scripture with the promises of God that go with it will give you a sure footing no matter what comes in life.

■ TO GROW AGAIN

Job 14:1-7: "At least there is hope for a tree: If it is cut down, it will sprout again, and its new shoots will not fail" (v. 7).

Recently I met two faithful believers in Jesus Christ, one an Asian, the other an African.

One has been out of prison only a year. He spent 18 years in that prison because he is a Christian and would not remain silent about it. What did hope mean to him in prison, as day after wearing day moved on? During the nights when he had no idea if he would see the light of freedom again did he think, "Oh, God, was I born for this?" Did he ever scream at God in despair? I have sometimes despaired over one short hour that did not please me or go the way I thought it should. I have anguished over circumstances, but not for 18 years. What does hope mean to a life like that?

The other man lost his precious child one week before I met him. His child is dead, and when he goes home that child will not run to greet him. He will not feel his arms around his neck. He will not hear the cry, "Daddy's home!" Does he find himself saying, "Oh, God, how can I have hope?"

Yet they serve and love God. These two men are proof that hope comes in the everyday struggles and the pain of living. These men are examples of the kind of hope that God is and God gives.

Thank you, Lord, for believers who are an example to me.

You may not have gone to prison for your faith. You may not have lost a child. Who do you know who has? With God's help, are you helping a tree cut down to sprout again?

■ LIFE STREAMS

Ps. 90:1-4: "Lord, you have been our dwelling place throughout all generations" (v. 1).

I was sitting in a little park in the city of Amsterdam. It's a place where five canals merge and then digress again to wander once more through the city, where people live and do their marketing, experience their joys, and face their tragedies. I watched the water moving at its own pace, neither hurrying nor slowing down, carrying with it some of the debris of people's living. Rising above the water were the gulls, sweeping and turning, settling again only to move on once more.

This seemed such a perfect picture of life, for life goes on just like the water in those canals. It moves regardless of what it carries along with it. It moves at its own pace, whether we float with it or occasionally, as the gulls do, rise above it. Like the water flowing from its source, we cannot start over again. But God who knows the source and outcome of every stream can be equally in charge of my steadily moving life.

There are pretty places on the canal. Wild roses grow along the bank. Other flowers that I don't know the names of bless me with their minute beauties.

Hope is along the banks of my life holding its beauties, if I could but see them. I only have to look.

Thank you, Lord, for the picture that, like the water, I too move with you and you hold me.

Are you watching for the minute beauties that God gives as life moves along? These are glimmers of life and hope. Cherish them.

■ ONE MORE TIME

John 3:16-21: "For God so loved the world that he gave his one and only Son, that whoever believes in him shall not perish but have eternal life" (v. 16).

If a child memorizes any verse of Scripture, it will probably be this one. Some are even encouraged—properly so—to put their own name in it. John 3:16 is called "the gospel in a nutshell." There is nothing confusing about this verse. It says clearly that those who believe will not perish.

Yet there comes again and again the doubt from people: "How can I really know? I hope I'll go to heaven," they say. That's the opposite to biblical hope which is based on a certainty, the certainty of the one who said, "Whoever comes to me I will never drive away" (John 6:37), and "In my Father's house are many mansions: if it were not so, I would have told you" (John 14:2 KJV).

Still, the next time you visit someone in the hospital or listen to people talking as they leave a church worship service, you may hear it again: "I hope I'm good enough to have eternal life." Then you will sigh, as perhaps God sighs, and quietly wonder how much clearer God can be. Patiently you tell the good news of eternal hope one more time.

 Thank you, Lord, for "the gospel in a nutshell." Help me never to tire of telling it again and again for those who have their doubts.

Do you have a systematic Bible memory program? Start one. Learn one verse per week. And, just as you have with John 3:16, attach your name to the verses.

■ YES

2 Cor. 1:18-21: "In him it has always been 'Yes' " (v. 19).

Always! It doesn't matter what the circumstances or how many promises, God's Word says, "Always." In him it has always been "yes." So I read my Bible with that word *yes* in my heart. "Thou wilt keep him in perfect peace, whose mind is stayed on thee" (Isa. 26:3 KJV)—yes. "I know that everything God does will endure forever; nothing can be added to it and nothing taken from it. God does it, so men will revere him" (Eccles. 3:14)—yes. "I am come that they might have life, and that they might have it more abundantly" (John 10:10 KJV)—yes. "And if I go and prepare a place for you, I will come again, and receive you unto myself" (John 14:3 KJV)—yes.

We can be certain with our yeses about God. We don't have to reply to God with a waffling, "Well, yes and no." On the authority of God's own Word we can say a resounding, clear and certain *yes*.

Yes, Lord, you are not unsure about yourself. Help me not to be either.

Learn to say yes in your daily Bible reading. Even write it in the margin of your Bible. See how personal God's Word is.

■ WELL DONE!

Matt. 25:19-21: "His master replied, 'Well done, good and faithful servant! You have been faithful with a few things; I will put you in charge of many things. Come and share your master's happiness!' " (v. 21).

What a glorious moment that will be, when we hear those words, "Well done, good and faithful servant. . . . Come and share your master's happiness!"

I was privileged to share in the memorial service for the pastor who helped me so much when I was a young Christian. He had been faithful, never wavering from his obedience to Christ and his proclamation of the gospel. He had time for me; he helped me; he cared about me. And as worshipers met in that church sanctuary and spoke of what he had done, I found myself thinking, "He is there in heaven; he is meeting the Lord he loved and served and longed to see, and he is hearing those wonderful words, 'Well done, good and faithful servant. . . . Come and share your master's happiness!' "

I, too, want to hear those words. For that, any sacrifice, any difficulties, any persecution or pain, will be worth it.

 Lord, a memorial service gives me still one more hint of the very best that's waiting. Thank you.

Is there someone today you should be helping? Will what you do be one more reason for the Master to say, "Well done"?

■ DASHED HOPES

Luke 24:17-21: "But we had hoped that he was the one who was going to redeem Israel. And what is more, it is the third day since all this took place" (v. 21).

They were disappointed. There's no doubt about that. Their faces were downcast, the Scripture says. They had hoped that Jesus was going to be the redeemer of Israel. They had put their trust in that, but it didn't happen—they thought. But it did happen, only not the way they had counted on.

That's a good reminder for us. We have our own idea of how our hopes should be met. We count on it, build our lives upon it. Then we, too, find ourselves with downcast faces. There are no restrictions on the way God will act. God will do what God has promised he will do in his time and in his way, not ours.

Have you lost hope? Do you feel it's the end, there can be no way that God can bring about what he so clearly seemed to be indicating? Walk down that road with those on the way to Emmaus. Sense with them what they were feeling. They had hoped. Now those hopes seemed dashed. Later they knew what the resurrection meant, and we know. Some days from now you may know all about your circumstances too.

Give me patience, Lord, to believe that your best is still coming.

List for yourself God's promises that you feel have not yet been answered. Check that list daily as you pray. Don't give up on God.

■ FAITHFULNESS MAY BE THREATENING

Matt. 5:11-12:   "Blessed are you when people insult you, persecute you and falsely say all kinds of evil against you because of me" (v. 11).

Insults and false statements, like water poured on the ground, cannot be recaptured. People say, "I want to be well liked and go to my grave with everybody thinking highly of me," but maybe that won't happen. Some people will say evil against us for no other reason than that faithfulness to God is in itself a threat to them, and they react. We don't cause the persecution, and we must not, but neither can we always stop it, because we cannot stop obeying God. We do our best and we wait, knowing that someday, perhaps not until Judgment Day, will people understand.

Robert Burton said, "Hope and patience are two sovereign remedies for all, the surest reposals, the softest cushions to lean on in adversity." Jesus is a cushion to lean on. Jesus was persecuted. The prophets were persecuted. The disciples were persecuted. We would like to avoid persecution, but when we think about it, if persecution comes, we're in great company.

 Lord, help me to be sure that I'm not causing a problem, but let me not assume that faithfulness will be respected by others.

Some of the most meaningful times of healing have come when one person asks another, "Is there something about me that is offending you?" That's hard to do, but it can clear the air. Should you be doing that?

Rom. 8:26-28: "And we know that in all things God works for the good of those who love him, who have been called according to his purpose" (v. 28).

There is more than hope in this verse; there is knowing. "We know," Paul said.

How can anybody know that "in all things God works for the good of those who love him?" Experience with God helps us to know. Listening to other Christians and watching God work in their lives helps. Believing God's promises helps too.

There is also knowing that comes from putting these verses with the two that go before, because they cannot be separated. If there is hope in Romans 8:28 it is because there is certainty in Romans 8:26 and 27.

There are no accidents in God's economy. He can use anything and everything that happens to you. That doesn't mean all things are good. All things are not good; some things are tragic. But God can work all things for good, and that's what makes the difference.

William Cowper said, "He has no hope who never had a fear." We may be weak, we may be frightened. But God's Spirit is our helper in prayer, and because he is, we know that God is working in our lives for good.

When bad things come, thank you, Lord, for the words "we know."

Do you tend to deny bad things, as some people do? Face them, knowing that these too are known to God. Love God, and see how this all works for good.

■ DECLARATION

Ps. 95:1-7: "Come, let us bow down in worship, let us kneel before the Lord our Maker" (v. 6).

When we worship God and offer thanks to God, we affirm our hope in him. Weekly worship offers the reaffirmation of that hope. Daily meditation and prayer responding to the Word of God is a commitment to our hope. It is an inward declaration of who God is and that our lives are committed to God.

Worship gives hope. Hope expresses itself in worship. When we drift away from daily prayer times, when we begin to substitute other things for weekly worship, we drift from our mooring—hope. If we avoid praise and adoration in worship, we begin to grow uncertain in our hope. If we miss worship, we miss the renewal of hope.

Hope comes when we genuinely are seeking the high and holy God and are adoring him. True worship brings a believer to the very throne of God, where God is central. In worship the focal point of our thinking is reaffirmed. Away from ourselves, we concentrate on God. And in that concentration and affirmation our hope is renewed and restored. We don't come to worship to find hope; we worship God, and in the worship hope is restored, renewed, and enlarged. So, "Come, let us bow down in worship, let us kneel before the Lord our Maker."

 Daily, Lord, I seek your face for the joy of knowing you. In so doing, my hope is renewed.

Who among your neighbors, friends, and relatives will you invite to church this Sunday? You cannot give them hope, but you can be God's instrument to bring them into a relationship of hope.

■ GROWING

Prov. 13:9-14:   "Hope deferred makes the heart sick, but a longing fulfilled is a tree of life" (v. 12).

Hope is living, and it gives health. Hope deferred allows illness and depression to come over a person. Like trees and flowers and grass, our hope will grow if we allow it. With each passing year the roots of hope go deeper, finding nutrients in the depth of God's goodness.

Hope grows because we who have it grow. Hope grows because God who gives it is alive, and although God never changes God's giving to us increases. The One who is the same yesterday, today, and forever gives more today than we were able to take in yesterday, and so we keep enlarging in our hope until we enter eternal hope and we don't need our present hope anymore. For "When he shall appear, we shall be like him; for we shall see him as he is" (1 John 3:2 KJV).

Samuel Johnson said, "The natural flights of the human mind are not from pleasure to pleasure, but from hope to hope."

 Dear Lord, may my hope, like a tree, grow with the roots going deeper and the branches giving more and more pleasure and shade to those around me.

Plant a tree in your yard and call it your hope tree. Watch it grow.

WALK INTO HOPE

Rom. 15:5-13: "May the God of hope fill you with all joy and peace as you trust in him" (v. 13).

On a quiet June afternoon I wandered alone along the nature trails at Sandringham, the estate of England's royal family. No one else was on the trails, just me, and a few red squirrels and crossbills. Tall Scotch pines, planted in 1850, filtered the sunlight, their branches caressing the occasional fleecy white clouds that passed by.

I had gone to see the royal home and the church; I stayed to enjoy the woods. It was an extra gift, something I hadn't expected. Each step took me deeper into the beauty of that ancient English woodland. Each step made me want to take one more.

Hope is like that. God's gift of hope comes to us usually when we're engaged in something else, not even looking for it, yet aware when we see it that it's a provision of the Father. Discovering hope, we find ourselves pulled into it, enjoying more of it, awed by the grace of it. Hope is personal. Others can hear about our hope, but each of us individually must take that walk into hope that defies either description or explanation but blesses beyond any measure we can put to it.

Lord, increase my trust, increase my hope, increase my joy and my peace.

Do you recall the last time you took a walk in a deep woods? Remember how the trees surrounded you and you felt drawn to go deeper and deeper? That's the way hope is. If you have forgotten, go for a walk in the woods today.

■ PROVEN

Ps. 119:113-120: "Sustain me according to your promise, and I will live; do not let my hopes be dashed" (v. 116).

As an adjunct faculty member at a college, teaching an occasional course in journalism, I find that one of the most difficult concepts to teach is that there is no such thing as objectivity. Students are taught that true reporters are objective; they are not. They are also taught that subjectivity cannot be proven or tested; they are wrong again.

Hope as a way of life is built on experiences, and experiences can be tested. But we've become so foolish about this and defensive that our hopes are quickly dashed by someone who says, "Well, you can be subjective if you want to about hope; I'm an objective person," as if somehow that's clearer, more scientific. We are taught that there is subjective truth and objective truth, and one is more valid than the other.

There is no such thing as truth that is not subjective. Anything observed, tested, heard, comes to the "me" through my subjective opinions, my sensations, my judgments. Don't let someone try to deny your hope who has no experience of it. They are not more objective or less subjective than you. They are only finding an explanation for their own inability to perceive.

Lord, thank you that my security and my hope is centered in you.

Determine now that you will never argue about the hope that is in you. Just live it.

■ SECURITY

Jer. 17:14-18:   "Do not be a terror to me; you are my refuge in the day of disaster" (v. 17).

In his book *The Kingdom of God*, John Bright said that Jeremiah never lost hope because he never lost God. It's interesting that in other translations the words of Jeremiah are: "Do not be a terror to me; you are my hope in the day of disaster." Hope and refuge are the same thing—a safe place, security, a place to go when there is terror.

When people are frightened, they seek different forms of security. Some go to alcohol or drugs. Some play "Let's Pretend" and keep busy partying, trying to forget. But the one who knows God knows that God is a refuge and a hope. When terrors come, and they do come, then we who trust God turn to the refuge and the hope we have. We are able to say with Jeremiah, "Heal me, O Lord, and I will be healed" (Jer. 17:14). For Jeremiah there was no question about it. And for emphasis he added, "Save me and I will be saved."

God is our surrounding fortress. Jeremiah knew that, and because he never lost God, he never lost hope.

Lord God, help me to know as Jeremiah knew the surrounding refuge that is you.

Commit to memory verses 14 and 17. When the day comes that you need these assurances, you will have them to cling to.

■ REVOLUTIONARY

2 Cor. 5:15-18: "If anyone is in Christ, he is a new creation" (v. 17).

The Christian faith is revolutionary, but not the way most people think. Our confused world sees Christians either as hoping for heaven and ignoring life now, or trying to bring about revolution by teaching that freedom in Christ is the same as political, social, and economic freedom.

But the Christian faith is revolutionary in a much deeper way. The One who can make all things new is the One who is God.

How can he make things new? With guns? By the ballot box? If so, we would not have needed Jesus. He gives new birth. He creates a brand-new person.

In submitting to Jesus Christ, we become free. This is incongruous to the one who does not understand it, but it is perfectly clear to the one who has been set free by Christ. And, having been set free, we can make real changes in this world, for we work with the One who entered it from the outside. We are directed by the Holy Spirit. We have hope beyond this world, and, as a result, we can offer hope to this world.

 Lord Jesus, help me to be as revolutionary as you through the power of your Holy Spirit in me.

Have you brought your voice to bear in revolutionary affairs? What kind of revolution should you be spreading?

HOPE, WHEN THE HEART IS RIGHT

2 Chron. 20:31-33:   "He did what was right in the eyes of the Lord" (v. 32).

The story of Jehoshaphat in 2 Chronicles 17-20 gives us hope. He was a man who didn't have much of an example in his father, Asa. Oh, Asa started out well enough, but he soon grew proud and did things his way, not God's way. But Jehoshaphat tried to be faithful, and throughout his lifetime he kept returning to the Lord, wanting to serve him. He made some bad alliances, yet God preserved him, especially in one of the major battles in which he could have been killed. In spite of some bad judgments, Scripture says he did right in the sight of the Lord. There is hope in those words, because the Lord knew Jehoshaphat's heart was right, in spite of his human frailties.

God can honor a person who sincerely wants to be obedient, even when in that sincerity that person strays and regrets it. God wasn't always pleased with what Jehoshaphat did, but it seems that God was basically pleased with him. It is pride, such as Asa had, that God opposes.

God knows our hearts just as he knew the heart of Jehoshaphat. If a person's heart is right toward God, there's hope.

 Lord, make my heart right toward you so that even when I make mistakes I can seek your forgiveness again.

If today you're being spiritually crippled by mistakes of the past, confess them, seek God's forgiveness, and go on. Scripture promises, "If we confess our sins, he is faithful and just to forgive us our sins, and to cleanse us from all unrighteousness" (1 John 1:9 KJV).

■ THE COMPANY OF HOPE

Eph. 1:15-23: "I pray also that the eyes of your heart may be enlightened in order that you may know the hope to which he has called you, the riches of his glorious inheritance in the saints" (v. 18).

All over the world there are people living by hope: hope in Christ, the hope taught by Christ, hope in the return of Christ. There is a lot of hope held by Christians in this world. They believe God.

When you come into the family of hope, you come into a group of people who support one another. They work together because they have the same basis for working, for believing. Their lives are founded on a certain hope. They are certain of the love, the nurture, the security, the promises and the gifts of God, and in the coming again of God's Anointed One, Jesus Christ.

Living and working by the same hope, the church around the world is salt and light. On the local level every believer unites with others to live out the hope. On the world level every believer unites with others in the larger community, sharing the faith. We are the company of hope. The eyes of our understanding have been enlightened. We know the hope of our calling, the riches of the glory of this inheritance in us, the saints.

 Thank you, Lord, for bringing me into this company of believers and this great, universally held hope.

Become acquainted through missionary letters or your denomination's mission board with missionaries elsewhere in the world. Communicate with them; learn something of the larger church. It will bless you and fill you with even more hope.

■ MOST MISERABLE

1 Cor. 15:12-19: "If only for this life we have hope in Christ, we are to be pitied more than all men" (v. 19).

We turn the pages of our news magazine and see starving children, ribs showing through their taut skin, and we say, "Pitiful people!"

Then we see on television a well-dressed, bejeweled businessman or preacher telling us, "You deserve. . . . Reach for it. . . . Don't wait. . . . Build now. . . . Eat. . . . Enjoy. . . . Take. . . . Consume." While we're shaking our heads and reaching to turn off the television set, we hear them referring to God and the teachings of Jesus and the Christian life in such statements as, "Name it; claim it." "A child of the King ought to go first class."

Theirs is a "grab now" gospel. They don't know about what will come later on, only what is now. Their lives deny the resurrection, even while they claim to believe it.

Many are suffering, not from their own doing but from the circumstances of politics, drought, and disease. Yet they are not the ones to be pitied "more than all men." Those words are reserved for people who think that all that matters is what they have now. They are the pitiful persons.

 Help me, Lord, to care for the real suffering of the world and not be captured by the teachings of those most to be pitied.

Am I giving my time and my resources to help those who are truly suffering in this world? Or am I concentrating my efforts on becoming one of those to be "pitied more than all men"?

■ EVERYWHERE

Eph. 4:3-7: "There is one body and one Spirit"
(v. 4).

God's church is growing. When the International
Congress for Itinerant Evangelists brought together
thousands of evangelists from 174 countries and
territories, the largest number of these evangelists
were from the Third World. Missionaries are going out
in ever-increasing numbers from developing countries,
as well as from the West. The average church member
in the world today is Asian or African and is under 25
years of age.

Every day thousands more around the world
become believers. Each week new churches are
started. They are of many denominations, ethnic
backgrounds, tongues. Yet all these who believe are
one in Christ. God is building his church, and for all
the individual human frailties in the church,
corporately it's strong.

The church is the body of Christ, the family of
hope. This is true whether the body members are in
local congregations, house churches, fellowship
groups, or are only a few who gather to pray together.

There is hope in every part of the world because
there are believers in every part of the world. They
are God's family.

 Thank you, Lord, for the church as a whole,
your body everywhere, and for the hope that
the church brings to every community.

**Since people from other countries live in almost every
community, what ministry of evangelism or
encouragement do you have with international
students or new residents in your community?**

■ CERTAINLY

Rom. 6:5-10: "If we have been united with him in his death, we will certainly also be united with him in his resurrection" (v. 5).

I waited a long week for the pathology report, and when it came the doctor interpreted the laboratory's findings. When he finished, I had assurance that the tissue was benign. I like it when a word like "benign" and a word like "certain" go together.

The Apostle Paul was able to use the word "certain" in an absolute way. "If we have been united with him in his death, we will certainly also be united with him in his resurrection." He could have said simply, "We will be united," but rejoicing in the certainty given by Jesus Christ to all who have died to sin in him, he was able to say enthusiastically, "We will certainly also be united with him."

So, on the basis of that statement, when I die with Christ I will be risen with Christ because there is no uncertainty to it. The Word doesn't say, "We might be united with him in his resurrection," or "We ought to be united." The Bible says, "We will certainly also be united."

There are not many certainties in life, but Paul shows us one of them in resurrection life, because it's a certainty promised by God. If we are now in Christ, then we are alive in him, and that life is forever.

O Holy Spirit, thank you for adding the emphasis "certainly."

Shut your eyes, lean back, think through the "if we have been." Be sure you have settled the "if," so that you can hold to the "will certainly also be."

■ I DIDN'T ESCAPE

Ps. 32:1-2: "Blessed is he whose transgressions are forgiven, whose sins are covered" (v. 1).

It was Halloween and we were just kids. Pushed by my friends, I climbed over a neighbor's back fence, grabbed a couple of tomatoes from his garden, and scrambled back before his angry dog reached me. Then we ran around to the front of the house, and my friends threw those tomatoes at the neighbor's front door. When he came out looking for us, we were hidden in the tall grass in the field across the street. I didn't get caught, and I was relieved, but I didn't escape the guilt. It's still with me, and if I could go back more than 40 years and say, "I'm sorry," I would.

Blessed also means happy, and David said, "Happy is he whose transgressions are forgiven, whose sins are covered." Are you happy because you know that your transgressions are hidden? Paul told us, "By grace are ye saved through faith; and that not of yourselves: it is the gift of God: not of works, lest any man should boast" (Eph. 2:8-9 KJV).

God gives the gift of faith, and faith brings with it salvation and hope. In Christ I did what I haven't been able to do with the man who lived in my old neighborhood. In Christ I've said, "I'm sorry," and asked God's forgiveness. No longer is there transgression still unforgiven. My sins are covered and I'm happy. That's the difference God makes.

Thank you, Lord, for forgiving me and covering my sins.

Are there people to whom you should say "I'm sorry"? Go to them, if you can, or write a letter. Get it settled. It will mean much to you.

WAGES AND THE GIFT

Rom. 6:20-23: "For the wages of sin is death, but the gift of God is eternal life in Christ Jesus our Lord" (v. 23).

We all know what wages are, and we all know what a gift is. Yet people still get mixed up when it comes to the wages of sin and the gift of life.

How can people get things backwards? When I go to work and get paid my just wage, that's not a gift. I worked for it. I deserve it, and I collect it. If I am concentrating on sin, working on sin, I receive the wages of sin, which is death—physical, emotional, spiritual. It is total death.

But the gift of God, which cannot be earned, is eternal life, total life. I can't work for a gift. If I could work for it, it wouldn't be a gift. One can never say to God, "You gave me the gift of death." God doesn't offer death; God offers life. Likewise, no one can say of life, "I earned it by my good works, my dedication, my attitude." It's a gift of God.

Still, you can't talk to people very long about spiritual things before you hear them talking about working for eternal life or wondering how God could "give" eternal death. People have always gotten the wages and the gift mixed up. Maybe they always will.

We can all receive the gift of life, and when we do, we can say, "Now I have hope, because I don't have the wages of sin anymore."

Thank you, Lord, for the clear distinction in Scripture between death and life.

Since we do good works in response to the gift of life, not to earn it, what good works are you doing now to thank God for the gift of life you received by faith in Jesus Christ?

■ HOW LONG?

Ps. 94:1-4: "How long will the wicked, O Lord, how long will the wicked be jubilant?" (v. 3).

The Rev. George Harper was looking forward to the return of Christ. He said, "The long night of world sorrow and sin has nigh run its course." So far as he was concerned, the world couldn't get any worse. It was as decadent as it could be. Surely Christ had to return. He said that in 1928.

And we've been saying the same ever since. "How long will the wicked be jubilant?" Can things get any worse? Have times ever been so bad? Yes, they have. The "good old days" were never really so good; we just have selective memories. If there are barbarians loose in the world today, there always have been. If there are corrupt business practices, that's not new. If there is murder and theft and sexual immorality, we may know more about it today because of better communications, but it was always there. Read histories of Europe or Asia in earlier centuries.

Things can get worse, and they may get worse. But in darkness, hope can shine even brighter. How long will the wicked be jubilant? Not long. Night won't last forever.

 I thank you, God, that reading or hearing about evil causes me to have a greater longing for you.

As a person of hope, are you serving on commissions to clean up pornography, a school board that looks at what children are being taught? Are you ministering in a rescue mission? Have you considered adopting an unwanted child? You have hope; you have something to give during these dark nights.

■ LEARNING HOW TO LEAN

Prov. 3:1-6: "Trust in the Lord with all your heart and lean not on your own understanding" (v. 5).

Are you disappointed about the turn of events in your life? Perhaps what you planned for or counted on didn't happen, and things are worse now than before. You had hoped that by now they would be so much better, but they aren't.

It's at times like these that faith is at its weakest. But it is also at times like these when we cling most to God's covenant with us. God said, "'I know the plans I have for you,' declares the Lord, 'plans to prosper you and not to harm you, plans to give you hope and a future'" (Jer. 29:11).

There are times in life, and this may be one of those times for you, when you can't lean on your own understanding, because your own understanding doesn't work. You have to lean on God. "In all your ways acknowledge him, and he will make your paths straight" (Prov. 3:6).

Hope isn't built on what we understand; hope isn't built on making our own paths straight. Hope is built on acknowledging and trusting God with all our heart.

Is your heart God's? If so, then even what appears as failure may be the start of God working out a plan for you.

Help me, Lord, to cling to the promise that you want good, not evil, for me.

If you have not yet committed to memory Prov. 3:5-6, now is the time to do it. It will come back to your mind when you need it most.

■ MOVING MOUNTAINS

Job 9:4-10:   "He moves mountains without their knowing it" (v. 5).

Do you have any mountains that need moving? When a mountain looms large and our path is blocked and we can't go over it and we can't go around, we want to sit down and weep. That's when we say, "I can't go on." That's when we cry in defeat, "There is no way around this problem."

Job tells us that God performs wonders that cannot be fathomed, miracles that cannot be numbered (v. 10). One of those wonders is moving mountains. Your mountain is huge, too big for you and your little pickax. But God is the God of miracles, so many that we can't even count them because we would run out of numbers. He can perform a wonder on your mountain, a miracle in your life.

If God can move a mountain without the mountain even knowing it, what can God do with your problem while you wait and watch and trust? Give God your mountain.

Almighty God, I place before you my own frustration at the mountain in my life. Will you remove it for me?

If you know someone who is facing a mountain today, pick up the telephone and call that person. Share this verse and give the gift of hope.

◼ TODAY

Luke 2:8-14: "Today in the town of David a Savior has been born to you; he is Christ the Lord" (v. 11).

Hundreds of years before Jesus was born, Isaiah said, "Therefore the Lord himself will give you a sign: The virgin will be with child and will give birth to a son, and will call him Immanuel" (Isa. 7:14).

Centuries went by, and people wondered, "When is he coming?" Especially they wondered when times were hard. Generations came and went, and still there was no Savior from God.

But God kept his Word. God keeps his Word now too. God's clock and calendar are not the same as ours. Jesus came in the fullness of time. In the same way your answers and mine also will come in the fullness of time.

"Today," the shepherds were told, "in the town of David a Savior has been born to you; he is Christ." No one had to wait any longer; it was today. A Savior, the Christ—today.

When God steps into history, it is in his time. You may be wishing for him to step into your life right now. But our hope is the same as the prophets' and the shepherds' and all others who waited then. Today, God says. Are you ready for God's *today* in your life?

 Help me, faithful Lord, to wait and not measure your involvement with me by my clock or calendar.

Can you recall a time in your life when, if God had answered what you wanted when you wanted, it would have been a terrible mistake? Aren't you glad God waited? Will you trust God now? If you will, tell God so.

■ THE CONTENT OF A LIFE

2 Tim. 2:20-22:   "In a large house there are articles not only of gold and silver, but also of wood and clay" (v. 20).

There is an idea, a rather foolish idea, that each individual life as well as all lives of humankind collectively somehow have an eternal meaning based upon their present meaning. In other words, what gives me meaning now is what will give meaning to me forever. So if it's pleasure or material things or titles or prestige, somehow that is carried over, and heaven will give me prestige, titles, pleasures or material things.

But into this kind of thinking comes Jesus Christ, and we understand that life is not based on the abundance of what we've collected. What Jesus offers is quite outside of all we've projected for ourselves.

How special is hope for Christians who are not constantly striving to project some eternal meaning out of what they have now or determining their own philosophy of heaven on the basis of what people think satisfies now. How different is hope for those who live in a love relationship with the Eternal. Meaning is given to them through Christ. Christ is the content of their lives. Christ is the all of their lives, and they live their lives out in Christ.

Lord Jesus, help me to keep my eyes focused on what is truly of value.

Look at your long-range goals. Analyze them. Are they God-given goals, pleasing to the Master? If they aren't, isn't it time for reevaluation?

■ WAITING

John 14:1-6:   "If I go and prepare a place for you, I will come back and take you to be with me . . . where I am" (v. 3).

It is love for his own that draws Jesus back to this earth again. He won't send a messenger; he's coming himself. "I will come again." Those are his words. He means them.

I travel a great deal in my work, and I miss my wife and home. As the days come closer to my return, I anticipate my homecoming more and more; my wife does too. But sometimes I get delayed. If I plan to be home on Friday and get delayed until Saturday, that's a long 24 hours, made longer because of the delay. But on occasion, when I suddenly discover that I can return one day sooner, that is a cause for rejoicing for both of us.

If that's true on our human level, how exciting, then, to anticipate the return of the Lord. Maybe he's delayed, but on the other hand, maybe he will return sooner than any of us anticipates.

Jesus is coming back. We are to wait for him, not just his expressions of love, though we rejoice in every one of those. Not just his gifts, though we're glad for them. We wait for him, and every action of his love and every gift that he gives only make us long the more for his personal return.

 Thank you, Lord Jesus, for the promise that "if I go, I will come again and take you to be with me." That gives me hope.

Do all of your friends and relatives know of your hope in the Lord's return? Isn't it time you told them what is really important to you?

Ps. 71:14-17: "But as for me, I will always have hope; I will praise you more and more" (v. 14).

We speak of losing hope, gaining hope, having hope. We even hope for hope. Sometimes people say, "I've given up all hope." Others, using a shipwreck analogy, cling to hope. Or they urge friends not to give up hope. Others hope against hope. There is false hope, and we are warned to guard against it. We hear of eternal hope, new hope, hoping and trusting, and we sing reverently of "Whispering Hope."

Is hope present tense, past tense, future? Is it something we had once or have now or will have someday? It is all of those, because hope is centered in God and God is past, present and future. He is the great I Am. He has no beginning and no end.

And because God is, our hope has neither beginning nor ending. The psalmist was correct: "I will always have hope; I will praise you more and more."

How could he know that? Because he knew he would always have God.

 Thank you, Lord, for the present tense of yourself. You are I Am, and your hope is always present.

Go through your prayer list of those who do not know the Lord. Put next to their names, "No God, no hope." Thinking about that will make a difference in your praying and in your witnessing.

■ A BIG ENOUGH SOUL

Mark 12:28-31: "Thou shalt love the Lord thy God with all thy heart, and with all thy soul, and with all thy mind, and with all thy strength: this is the first commandment" (v. 30 KJV).

When God breathed into his crowning creation, humankind, God made Adam a living soul—not a small part of a soul, but a soul big enough for the Spirit of God to dwell in. God's breath came into man.

Jenkin Lloyd Jones said, "You cannot put a great hope into a small soul." He was right. You cannot. A soul grows smaller and smaller from self-worship, worry, lack of dependence on God. In touch with God's Word our souls expand with more and more awareness of God.

Sometimes we ask ourselves, "How can I have a greater hope?" Maybe the question should be, "How's your soul?" A big soul can contain a big hope because a big soul can receive more and more of the inbreathing of God, and God is hope.

Dear God, you gave me a soul, and I'm to love you with all of it. Help me to do so.

In the morning ask yourself, "How will I find a way today to love God with all my heart, my soul, mind and strength, and my neighbor as myself?"

■ BAD GRAMMAR

Ps. 147:7-11: "The Lord delights in those who fear him, who put their hope in his unfailing love" (v. 11).

We've all had it happen: someone comes to us in a patronizing way as we're going through a difficult time, and declares, "Now you must try to have hope. If you hope enough, maybe your wish will come true." These people mean well, but they're not biblical.

People talk of hope as if it's only a verb. But in the Bible, hope isn't only a verb, it's also a noun. Hope is not only what we do, it's what we have. It seems that people not only need to understand hope, they need a good grammar lesson too.

If hope is only what we're able to do, then the poet was correct when he said, "Hope springs eternal in the human breast; man never is, but always to be blest." The hope we possess in Christ is not just a wish or something we try for; it's a reality, a possession that we know and hold.

 Thank you, Lord of love, that there is more to hope than my trying. Thank you for hope that is built on you, on who you are, on what you've said and what you've done.

Assess the hope you have now. Clarify it in your thinking so that when tough times come—and they will—you can recall your reason for holding on and at the same time have an answer for those who still need to understand what hope is.

HOPE LIST

1 Sam. 7:7-9: "Do not stop crying out to the Lord our God for us, that he may rescue us" (v. 8).

It was late, the prayer rally having ended close to 10:00 P.M. As the headlights of our car pierced the darkness, my wife and I began to talk about what had happened that evening. At the conclusion of the service everyone gathered in small groups to pray. They were different ages, different denominations, but all one in Christ and of one mind in their praying. Many had a personal list of "hoped for" answers: the wife whose husband is not a believer, the father whose son seems intent on continuing his rebellion, the young woman whose sister left home and every semblance of godliness. There was hope in that room that evening, and we were still feeling the glow of it many miles down the road.

"Pray without ceasing" (1 Thess. 5:17 KJV), Scripture says, and we knew those people would.

Years ago there was a lot of hope in the requests of the people to Samuel too. "Do not stop crying out to the Lord our God for us, that he may rescue us." They needed God and knew it. There is a lot of hope where people pray together.

As we drove home that evening, my wife and I sensed how near we felt to God because we had been with people praying.

Thank you, Lord, for fellow believers with whom we can pray.

If you do not have a prayer partner or a prayer fellowship, find one. You will be blessed.

■ NO MORE TEARS

Rev. 21:1-4: "He will wipe every tear from their eyes. There will be no more death or mourning or crying or pain" (v. 4).

It was a simple graveside ceremony. She had lived a long life, and not many friends or family members were left. Those who were there, lost in their own memories, listened as words were said about this life that was lived. And there were tears—tears because she was gone, tears because of the pain that she had known in her life, especially toward the end, tears because things did not work out in her life the way she would have had them work out, tears for disappointments.

That's the way things are for us now. But someday God, in his tenderness, will wipe away every tear, and there will be no cause for tears, because there will be no more mourning and no more pain. We all groan and suffer because of the corruption, the evil, the sin that grips this world. But someday the old will pass away. Heaven waits. That's not an empty hope or wish, but a reality. Jesus said, "In my Father's house are many mansions: if it were not so, I would have told you. I go to prepare a place for you" (John 14:2 KJV).

At the graveside, when we reach into our pocket for a handkerchief to wipe away another tear, those words are vivid and real.

 Thank you, Lord, even for pain and sorrow which serve as a reminder that it will not always be so.

The next time you attend a funeral, don't try to disguise death. It is real, it is painful. Let that pain be a reminder of the day when there'll be no more pain or sorrow or tears.

■ NOT THE TEMPORARY

2 Cor. 4:13-18: "So we fix our eyes not on what is seen, but on what is unseen. For what is seen is temporary, but what is unseen is eternal" (v. 18).

Today there's a worship of the physical to the point that goes beyond health. If we don't look a certain way or have a certain body weight, we are embarrassed.

There is a worship of things too. Turn on the television set some night and you'll find someone pitching a surefire method of turning 10 dollars into a million. On display are photos of successful people standing next to yachts, big cars, mansions, all to capture the eye. Go to a high-priced conference on investments or franchises or pyramids, and you will hear things like, "Earn an income to fit your wants." Why doesn't someone hold a conference on restraining your wants to fit your income?

Paul had to deal with that too. He had to remind believers that we fix our eyes not on what is seen but on what is unseen, the eternal, not the temporary.

Probably one of the best things that could happen is for people to get all that they dream about so they'll soon prove to themselves how empty all that is. Then when they have everything piled high around them, they might turn and look for what is truly real.

 Lord, without neglecting my physical body and temporal things, help me to keep my eyes on the eternal.

One of the best places for teaching the difference between what is temporary and what is eternal is in the younger classes at Sunday school or vacation Bible school. Have you volunteered to teach such a class and get children's eyes correctly focused early in life?

■ HOPE FOR A CLAY POT

Jer. 18:1-5: "So the potter formed it into another pot, shaping it as seemed best to him" (v. 4).

There's hope for a clay pot as long as it is still pliable. Any defect or flaw can be remedied. The potter can rework the clay in his hand and put it back on the wheel. But if the clay is hardened, resistant to any change, and there's a defect or a flaw or a weakness in its composition, what can the potter do but to throw the pot into the corner?

Scripture says, "A wicked man hardens his face" (Prov. 21:29 KJV). And the statement is made in Prov. 29:1, "He, that being often reproved, hardeneth his neck, shall suddenly be destroyed, and that without remedy."

God doesn't want to throw anyone into the corner. God didn't create us for that; God didn't empty himself and come to earth in Christ Jesus for that. Our Lord didn't go to the cross for that; he didn't rise from the dead for that. God doesn't want broken pots in the corner. Our hope is not, "I hope that God doesn't throw me into the corner." Our hope is that we remain open to the working of God in our lives, responding to God, allowing the Master Potter to do the beautiful work that he desires to do in each one of us.

Lord, keep me pliable. Do your perfect work in me.

If you can find a cracked and broken old clay pot, put it somewhere where you'll see it every day. On it place the words, "Not me, Lord."

■ IMPOSSIBLE

Gen. 18:10-15: "Is anything too hard for the Lord? I will return to you at the appointed time" (v. 14).

I was finishing my college work, longing to go to seminary in the fall, but I needed four courses in my major to complete my degree. I could take two in the spring and two in the summer. The problem was, when it was time to enroll in my courses in the spring, I didn't know which two classes would be offered in the summer. Also, I needed to work full time in the summer to pay for my tuition. But believing the words, "Is anything too hard for the Lord?" I went ahead and signed up "blindly" in the spring.

Later, the summer courses in my major were listed—the exact two I needed for graduation. Also they were offered not during the day but on alternate evenings. Then my part-time employer asked if I could work full time that summer and also if I would be willing to start an hour earlier and then leave work an hour earlier in the afternoon. This gave me a full-time job, a chance to study before my classes, and the courses I needed for my degree in time to go to seminary. Is anything too hard for the Lord?

When we face the impossibles of our lives, we can do what Sarah did and laugh or we can take God at his word: Is anything too hard for the Lord?

Help me, Lord, to realize that you are not limited by my limits.

Take the most impossible situation you are facing right now. Bring it to the Lord with the statement, "Nothing is too hard for you." Present it to God, then watch for God's fulfillment at the appointed time.

■ SECURE

Ps. 16:1-9: "Therefore my heart is glad and my tongue rejoices; my body also will rest secure" (v. 9).

No night is like any other. Each is different; each has a face of its own. There are so many nights in our lives. The happy nights of lovers touching, discovering, secure. The nights of a child, sometimes peaceful, sometimes frightening, depending on the noises, the shadows, and who is near to hold her. Lonely nights when no one is there, and we want someone to be there even when we don't know who that someone is or even know how that someone could help. Nights of weakness, the slow moving nights, when we don't know what is happening to our minds or inside our pain-wracked bodies; it is so frightening.

But into our nights God comes. The psalmist said, "My body also will rest secure." Other translations phrase it, "rest in hope." Security and hope fit together.

Into our nights God comes because God wants to. God has always wanted to. God waits for entrance into all of our nights, and brings hope. God brings security. With hope and security in our hearts, we can say, "Welcome, night; I do not fear you."

Thank you for hope and security when I am frightened in my darkest nights.

What Scriptures do you keep by your bedside for the nights when you cannot sleep? Make such a collection, perhaps on little cards, so that Ps. 16:7 and 9, as well as other verses, will be promises for you.

GOLD

Job 31:24-29: "If I have put my trust in gold or said to pure gold, 'You are my security' " (v. 24).

I like to teach college-age young people, and sometimes in a class or a retreat or in personal conversation I'll make a statement such as, "Wouldn't it be a terrible thing if you came to the end of your life and all that could ever be said of you was that you earned lots of money? What a waste!" Yet so many young people and their parents are challenged more by accumulating money and what money can buy than by anything else.

Job had a lot of money. He understood what gold was for. When it was all taken from him and he asked God, "Why?" it was because he knew, and he knew that God knew, that gold was never what he worshiped. His confidence was not in gold. If it had been, he would have been rightfully judged.

All around us are unbiblical voices telling us to put our confidence in gold, hope in gold, trust in gold—in short, worship gold. Any substitute for God will do, and if gold appeals, Satan will stress gold. He doesn't want people worshiping God. Job's concern was not to have more gold; Job's concern was to have more of God. What's your concern?

 As it was with Job, dear God, so it is with me. I know I'll be judged on the basis of where I put my trust.

Make Job your model regarding gold, not worshiping it if you have it, nor craving it if you don't.

■ PRISONER OF HOPE

Zech. 9:9-13: "Return to your fortress, O prisoners of hope" (v. 12).

It's an interesting difference. I have visited prisoners in penitentiaries, state institutions, city jails, even ships' brigs, and almost without exception all have declared their innocence. They were framed; somebody did much worse but got away with it. They wanted to get out. But I have also been to old forts, castles in England and Europe—places where people wanted to stay. They felt secure.

Zechariah was urging people to return to their fortress, where they could be prisoners of hope. He was talking to "prisoners," not the kind who wanted to get out but the kind who needed to stay in. There's security within the boundaries of hope, trust that God is going to do battle on our behalf.

What kind of prisoner are you—one who wants to get out or one who wants to be in? It's interesting that God's prisoners—prisoners of hope—are those who are freed from waterless pits. We aren't free when we are outside the walls; we're in waterless pits under the baking sun. There is no refreshment there. Why do so many people call it freedom to be outside in waterless pits when the real freedom is inside the fortress of God as a prisoner of hope?

Lord, I choose to be a prisoner of hope. Thank you for that security.

Have you ever thought of "adopting" a prisoner, someone to write to and visit? You'll not only give him or her an understanding of real freedom, you'll gain a greater understanding of imprisonment.

■ BRUISED

Isa. 42:1-9: "A bruised reed he will not break, and a smoldering wick he will not snuff out" (v. 3).

She had been at the peak of popularity, a Miss America contestant who traveled the country speaking to large groups and being feted. Then she fell off her glittering mountain into bad marriages, ugly divorces, alcoholism. Finally, near death, she found Christ and had a new reason for being, a life with real meaning at last. When I met her, I found myself wondering, "Why does it take so long?" And as I watch others going down the same path, I keep thinking, "Must they go that far? Must they be that hurt? Must they experience that much pain before they discover where there is hope?"

Sometimes we wonder, do we even have a right to hope? But then we read the blessed news given to us in Isaiah 42, and we know that God will take even a broken reed and bind it up. God will take a smoldering wick and fan it into flame. That's our hope, the blessed news of the redeeming and restoring God, no matter how bruised the reed or smoldering the wick.

 Thank you, God, for redemptive hope no matter what.

Is there someone in your life you've given up on? God hasn't given up on that person. See that person as a broken reed, a smoldering wick, and lay claim to God's promise.

■ HE DID IT

Heb. 7:11-19:   "And a better hope is introduced, by which we draw near to God" (v. 19).

God is not helplessly frustrated by our sin. God's not wringing his hands saying, "What can I do?" God is not exasperated by our inability to live by the commandments, to be what we were created originally to be. God entered history in Jesus Christ, providing a work of redemption that we could not provide ourselves nor gain through keeping the law. What had to be done, God had to do, because in our sinful state we could do nothing on our own but perpetuate that sinful state. The unclean cannot cleanse itself. It must be cleansed. So God did it.

God entered this world to cleanse. That's not a negation of our own ability or value; that's putting the emphasis where it should be—on God. And because we believe in Jesus and his atoning work, we also have hope in the results of that work, the holiness, the sanctification. It stems from our obedience to the One who gives it. We have a reason for our hope. We can have hope because we believe what God has said about us, and we believe in what he has done for us through Jesus Christ. He is our better hope. We can draw near to God.

Thank you, God, that what I could not do for myself you did for me in Christ Jesus.

Salvation by faith alone is followed by good works. What good work today does your salvation move you to do?

■ ENCOURAGED

2 Cor. 7:10-13: "By all this we are encouraged" (v. 13).

As I was unpacking in my hotel room in Taiwan, there was a knock on my door. It was the room boy carrying a pitcher of ice water. He smiled, introduced himself, and said, "You want beautiful, young girl, you ask me."

"No," I said.

Confused but obedient, he left.

I had a dinner meeting that took most of the evening, but later a great sense of loneliness overwhelmed me. I had been traveling through Asia; this was the third city with one more to go before I could return home. I had no desire to wander the streets; the novelty of people and shops had worn off long ago. Instead I sat in my room feeling sorry for myself.

I went to sleep with this depression, and in the morning in my prayer and Bible-reading time I stumbled on, or was led to, 2 Corinthians 7. Paul's words spoke to me: "By all of this we are encouraged."

Paul was "greatly encouraged," he said in verse 4. That prayer and Bible reading time brought me encouragement too. But I did think, "Would I have had hope or encouragement if I'd had guilt? Could I have expected anything from God?" That time with God was a learning time, a time to discover what Paul knew—that deliverance, like faith, like hope, is a gift from God. And I was encouraged.

 Thank you, Lord, for your encouragement even in discouraging and lonely times.

Ask God to protect you when you are traveling or are alone. Ask God to keep you close to himself.

■ WITHOUT WARNING

Ps. 33:18-22: "May your unfailing love rest upon us, O Lord, even as we put our hope in you" (v. 22).

Nothing is ever certain. Danger can come without warning. But the psalmist was correct: "The eyes of the Lord are on those who fear him" (v. 18).

I thought of that one day when I was on a flight over the coast of Italy. It was extremely smooth and comfortable, when suddenly, without warning, the plane dropped more than a thousand feet. The woman next to me had a drink in her hand. When we went down, her hand holding the glass went too, pulling the glass away from the liquid, which seemed to stay in the air for a few seconds before it splashed all over her.

No one was ready for that drop. There was no time to build up hope, no time to turn to God's Word, no time to pray—just enough time to be frightened.

As on that airplane ride, none of us can always know ahead of time what we're going to go through. But our hope is in God when we are not afraid, and our hope is in him when we are afraid. Hope is the one constant.

 Thank you, Lord, that hope is based not on conditions—good or bad— but on your protection.

If you are the type of person who turns to God only in a crisis, change that now. Let God show you the real meaning of hope in the quiet good times when you can absorb it. Then it will be there when the sudden drops in your life occur.

■ LOVE STORY

Acts 2:22-28: "I saw the Lord always before me" (v. 25).

He was a young, newly married, Chinese Christian. As we rode to Hong Kong's airport together, we talked about our families. I asked him how he met his wife. He smiled and said, "We met praying for China." Then he explained, "We were part of a group that was to visit the mainland, and we met to pray. Then, on the tour, we discovered how much we cared about the same things. We had the same concern to take the gospel to China, and our love story began."

That love story has continued, but tragically many other love stories have not. A love story begins, then almost imperceptibly it starts to take on new chapters, painful chapters, and the story ends.

David said, "I saw the Lord always before me." And because he did, he could add, "Therefore my heart is glad and my tongue rejoices; my body also will live in hope" (v. 26). The key to a love story that continues and deepens is these two emphases—the Lord always before me and the glad heart that gives hope.

 Thank you, Lord, for love stories that go on and deepen because both husband and wife see the Lord always before them.

If there are questions or problems in your marriage, begin the healing by bringing first yourself, then your spouse, before the Lord.

■ NO SIMPLE ANSWERS

Job 8:8-13: "They wither more quickly than grass. Such is the destiny of all who forget God" (vv. 12-13).

A church leader once announced that if his children turned away from God, he would leave the ministry, because Scripture speaks of "governing his own house." I could not say that. I've seen too many families where the parents are faithful and so are all the children except one. That child, in his need to be independent, declares his freedom from God. Sometimes that rebellion goes on and on, even into adult years. Parents blame themselves, they cry to God, they would do anything for the prodigal, but like the father in the story Jesus told, they can only wait. Every effort to reach out sends the renegade into greater spasms of rebellion.

What causes this? Why does it happen to some but not to others? Any simple answer is wrong, because any simple answer is incomplete. If there were easy answers, they would have been found in the many sleepless nights. Parents are obliged to go on, taking life one day at a time.

Each child makes his own selection; each has his own filtering system, rejecting what he will, keeping what he will accept. Parents cannot quit, shrink into the corner or fold under the term *failure*. Instead we look to God for forgiveness and unchanging love.

Thank you, Lord, for your love and assurance to us and to our children.

We are holders of hope and hope bringers. Is there a suffering mother, father, or prodigal child that you can help today?

■ ARE YOU GOING NOWHERE?

Eccles. 9:3-8: "Anyone who is among the living has hope—even a live dog is better off than a dead lion!" (v. 4).

This is a strange verse of Scripture, but no verse is in the Bible accidentally. All Scripture is given by inspiration of God, so God wanted this verse here. Maybe God wanted it here for you.

There is hope among the living. Sometimes we look at the dead and think "how peaceful," because our anxiety is so great. But there's hope for the living; there is no hope for the dead. They are what they are—redeemed or lost. There can be no change.

"But," you may be saying, "though I'm alive I might as well be dead; I'm going nowhere." Are you convinced that you can do nothing more with your life? Then turn to God and honestly say, "I can't do anything with my life. I am turning everything that I have, all that I have done, and all that I hope to do over to you."

Confess that you are sinful. Ask for forgiveness and claim the promise "that whosoever shall call on the name of the Lord shall be saved" (Acts 2:21 KJV). That's a life-giving promise. Take at face value the promise in Scripture: "I have come that they may have life, and have it to the full" (John 10:10).

 Thank you, Lord, that when I feel that I can't do anything, I am brought to realize that you can do everything.

Write down on slips of paper the troubles that are burdening you. Put them in a dish or a bowl and in prayer present that entire collection to God. Then put them in the garbage where you won't have to see them anymore.

■ WHOSE LIMITS?

Psalm 23: "Even though I walk through the valley of the shadow of death, I will fear no evil, for you are with me" (v. 4).

Perhaps you have been thinking about suicide. Don't be upset that you have entertained that thought, but consider for a moment. What will you gain? What release will be given? Will you escape from the pressures that are upon you? God knows all of those pressures. God knows the fiery furnace you're in, just as God knew the one the three friends of Daniel were in. Your prison, like Paul's, may be awful beyond description, but God was with Paul in prison. God is with you too. To take matters into your own hands is to say, "God must release me from where I am, or I will release myself."

It would be a simple matter for God to release you, but he hasn't. Are you smarter than God? "But I can't take anymore," you say. Can't you? Have you decided your limits and God's? The psalmist went clear to the valley of death in his misery but was able to say, "Even though I walk through the valley of the shadow of death . . . you are with me."

Despair can drive you to the source of all hope. You may be closer than you think to God's deliverance and victory.

Help me, Lord, like the psalmist, to know that you walk with me even through the shadows.

If you are entertaining death thoughts, find a Christian counselor or pastor or other mature believer who can pray with you and encourage you from God's Word. Never try to go through a valley alone.

WITH YOUR EYES OPEN

Job 11:13-20: "You will be secure, because there is hope; you will look about you and take your rest in safety" (v. 18).

We were in Sussex, England, holding classes for Christian writers. At the end of the day, as the last workshop ended, someone turned on a taped television interview with David Watson. This effective, faithful clergyman was talking about faith and trust and having hope. Yet we knew that since that taping he had died of cancer. He died hoping for a cure.

Cynics can't understand that kind of hope; they rebel against God. But believers don't; they hope in God. They surrender and trust. Some people die with clenched teeth and curses. Believers, true believers like David Watson, die with hope.

Job understood that. He spoke of devoting the heart to God, to lift up our faith without shame, to stand without fear. He wrote as one who had his eyes open ("looking about," he phrased it), taking rest in safety. David Watson was looking about with his eyes open, telling those interviewing him what it was like to be dying. What came through so clearly was what it was like to be dying in hope. Only one who has lived with eternal hope can die with eternal hope.

Lord, I live in hope now. Help me to know how to die in hope.

Come to terms with death while you are in your full strength and health. It will give you a balance, a perspective. Know how you want to face this adventure.

■ HOPE AND JUSTICE

Mic. 6:6-8: "He has showed you, O man, what is good. And what does the Lord require of you? To act justly and to love mercy and to walk humbly with your God" (v. 8).

When we treat God casually, when we have a buddy-buddy, arm-around-the-shoulder, Jesus-as-best-friend relationship and lose the wonder of who God is, we also lose hope. Wonder and hope are intertwined. Why? Because wonder causes us to be in awe, to bow the head, to drop to our knees, to express our limits and God's limitless strength. The more the wonder of that grasps our souls, the more reason we have for hope.

When we treat God casually, we also take hope away from God's creation. A low view of God generates a low view of God's creation. A high view of God gives a high view of God's creation. Humankind is the crowning part of God's wonderful creation, but when we do not recognize God we do not recognize the value of human beings.

Justice begins with walking humbly with God. Our world needs justice, and our world will have more hope for justice as they see us bowing the knee before God and walking humbly with him.

 Lord, help me to see the relationship between a high view of you and a high view of other people.

Perhaps there's not much hope in the world because there's not much awe of God in the world. What can you do to change that?

STANDING FIRM

James 1:12-18: "Blessed is the man who perseveres under trial, because when he has stood the test, he will receive the crown of life" (v. 12).

We don't like it, but we find ourselves on every page of the Bible. For just as God shows us who he is and what he does, God also shows us who we are and what we do. We wish we could see the one and not the other. Life doesn't work that way; it never has.

James understood that. He knew in the first century that people did what people have always done. Temptation comes. People dream about the delight of it, savor it, then act on it. And when the result of it comes, the punishment, people blame God. James understood that God doesn't tempt anybody; only the good and the perfect gifts come from the good and perfect God. So, led by the inspiration of the Holy Spirit, James shows us the opposite side of that drifting into sin. Happy, blessed, are those who persevere under trial, because having stood—and it's hard to stand when the pressures are pushing—they will receive the crown of life.

God has promised the crown, but not to those who slip and slide and give in and then whine, "It's all God's fault." No, the promise is to those who stand firm and love God. The one has no hope unless he turns; the other, standing firm, has a lot of hope.

 Dear God, you never said it would be easy. Help me to plant my feet and stand the test.

The next time you take your children or grandchildren to the seashore, stand with them in the waves. Let the push and pull of the sea be an illustration of this passage. They'll never forget it.

GOD'S POEM

Eph. 2:1-10: "For we are God's workmanship, created in Christ Jesus to do good works" (v. 10).

When I talk to young poets about their craft, I encourage them in the refining of each line—the balance, the symmetry, the cadence. There is no excess verbiage in a poem; it is carefully constructed so that its content as well as its feeling touches the soul. In short, it has both a head meaning and a heart feeling. It's rich in its depth. One can read a true poem again and again and feel as well as learn.

That's exactly what Paul is talking about when he refers to us as God's workmanship; we are like a poem carefully crafted by God. When I see myself as a carefully created work, a product of God's skill, I have a whole new understanding of who I am in Christ Jesus and my value to God.

I'm a poem. God didn't throw out sloppy, unthought-out prose when he created you and me; God crafted a poem. And all who see that poem know that God did it. We are for God a poem to the world. God enjoyed his craftsmanship. The world sees that craftmanship, and you know that God who was so careful in his workmanship will not toss it aside. God will display his work proudly.

Thank you, Lord, for the careful craftsmanship that you put into me.

Read good poets. See how they have crafted their lines. Note what the reading does to you in your heart and soul. Then recognize that you are God's poem for the whole world to read.

■ NOT SUPERIOR

Dan. 12:8-10: "But the wicked will continue to be wicked" (v. 10).

Don't laugh at these words of Daniel. They aren't redundant; they're profoundly wise, given to him by the person Daniel describes as the "one who looked like a man."

The wicked continue to be wicked. That's so profound we miss the truth of it. So many of us, for some reason, expect the wicked to be good. "Why do people do that?" we ask. We expect morality, decency, goodness. Why? Can those who reject God act like those who accept him? Can those who have not the gift of life act like ones who do? Can those who have no hope live like those who do have hope? And if there is no life, no hope, no joy, no peace, or any of the gifts of God, what is left?

Daniel's words are not redundant to make us giggle. They are stated for emphasis. There is a great distinction between the "many purified, made spotless and refined" and the wicked. That's not a point of superiority or inferiority; it's an explanation of what is. The pure will not act wickedly, not if they're truly pure. The wicked cannot be pure, because they are wicked. The role of the pure is not to boast in it but to recognize God in it, then carry the message of God to the wicked.

 Help me, Lord, not to condemn or criticize but to reach out lovingly to the wicked who know no other way to live.

Be a Christian who takes the gospel into the world, for there are many in the world who have a longing. They know the difference between wickedness and purity too.

■ THE SOURCE OF HAPPINESS

Ps. 38:9-15: "I wait for you, O Lord; you will answer, O Lord my God" (v. 15).

God knows our longings, our sighings. He understands the pounding heart. God knows what it is to be left alone. We say with David, "I wait [or hope] for you, O Lord."

Philo of old understood it, too, not from a biblical perspective but from a purely human perspective: "Hope is the source of all happiness . . . none is to be considered a man who does not hope in God."

What are we, then, if we don't have hope? Philo understood that somehow we are less than what we were created to be, less than human, if we do not have hope. For without hope there is no source of happiness.

David's life, Philo's life, your life, my life, prove it again and again. When our hearts pound, when our longings are great, when our sighings overwhelm us, when we are alone, then we need hope. "I wait for you, O Lord." Then comes the assurance, "You will answer."

And God does.

Then comes happiness.

Lord, you are hope, and that hope is the source of my happiness.

Notice in reading the classics or even contemporary novels how much the human emotions point out scriptural truths. It will give you a good understanding of where people are and a way of offering hope to them.

COURAGE TO VENTURE FAR

Ps. 57:1-3: "I will take refuge in the shadow of your wings until the disaster has passed" (v. 1).

These are the words of one who knew the need for refuge, to flee for protection as chicks do under the wings of a hen until they can venture out again. They can't stay under the wings; they have to scratch and stretch and grow, but the refuge is always there.

Our refuge is in God. Trust in God's security gives courage to those who suffer for the faith in the restrictive places of the world. But that same trust may be lacking where Christians have freedom. The church seems to be growing fastest in the suffering places of the world, but fading in the places where there is ease. Jesus told his disciples, "Blessed are you when people insult you, persecute you and falsely say all kinds of evil against you because of me. Rejoice and be glad, because great is your reward in heaven, for in the same way they persecuted the prophets who were before you" (Matt. 5:11-12).

If you have ever wondered what that means, talk to many in the Third World where the gospel is spreading and compare what they tell you to what you see in the developed nations where the gospel does not seem to be spreading so fast. God has suffering people, but that's the point—they are in God's care. Their hope is in God's refuge, and with that hope they can venture far and accomplish much.

 Lord, thank you for those who are faithful to you in spite of persecution and suffering.

If people with little freedom are speaking out boldly for Christ, how are you using the larger freedom that you have?

■ ASKING QUESTIONS

John 12:31-35: "But I, when I am lifted up from the earth, will draw all men to myself" (v. 32).

Recently pollster George Gallup Jr., speaking to a group of international reporters, said, "People in many nations appear to be searching with a new intensity for spiritual moorings. One of the key factors prompting this search is certainly a need for hope in these troubled times."

What George Gallup found is what each of us will find as we also ask people questions, even asking those who seem to have their lives in order. Listen to their problems, and you'll soon sense a search for certainty, a need for hope.

Jesus asked questions of people and responded to their need for hope. Sometimes it was a hope for healing, a hope to be fed, a hoping for the restoration of a dead loved one; and there was always the hope for forgiveness, the assuaging of guilt, the assurance of cleansing.

Asking questions is a good thing. It leads to finding out what people are searching for. It gives us an opportunity to tell about the One who wants to bring people to himself. Jesus told those around him, "When I am lifted up from the earth, I will draw all men to myself."

Questions open the door for lifting up Jesus. Questions lead to expressed needs. Those needs are met when Jesus Christ is lifted up.

Lord, help me to lift up Jesus and not be quiet about him.

Who have you asked questions of today? Who are you sensitive to? And have you presented Jesus to that person?

■ AN EXAMPLE OF GREATER GLORY

2 Cor. 3:7-12: "Since we have such a hope, we are very bold" (v. 12).

Never before in the history of the world had so many nations gathered under one roof in one place at one time. It was the International Conference for Itinerant Evangelists. In Amsterdam, in July 1986, evangelists from 174 nations and territories, more than are members in the United Nations, gathered to equip themselves to be even better at their task of calling men and women to saving faith in Jesus Christ. They came with great boldness; they left with an even greater boldness. They learned from each other, exchanged ideas, prayed together, studied. Their average age was 31—their best years of ministry still ahead of them. They came with excitement, for in some of their countries the church is growing faster than the population.

They are an example of what Paul was talking about, not of a fading glory but of a greater glory which lasts. They are believers with an unfading gospel to proclaim, and the results are even now being felt as some of their ministries have tripled and quadrupled as a result of that great conference. Believers are going everywhere to tell the good news.

We are bold for Christ when we have hope in Christ. Hope possessors are people with a message to tell. They are the people of the unfading glory, and their news is unfading too.

Lord, make me bold for Christ because I have hope also.

Are you bold for Christ? Will you pray today to be so?

■ OUR FATHER

Matt. 6:7-13: "Our Father in heaven, hallowed be your name" (v. 9).

One of the great rewards of traveling in various countries of the world is the pleasure of praying with fellow believers. The family of faith is universal. There is not a continent or country in the world where the gospel has not been heard in some way, and in almost every part of the world there are now believers. And they pray.

The Korean church is growing because the people pray. The church in China has expanded mainly because the people pray. The fastest growing churches in the world are in Brazil and Argentina and Nigeria because the people pray. In Eastern Europe, though there cannot be much outward show of religious faith, the people pray. And to pray with them is a blessing beyond description, for all culture and custom is pushed aside when people together pray to "Our Father," with the emphasis on *our*.

For God is ours. God is greater than any nation, greater than politics, greater than our economic systems. There is a oneness in the family of faith, and barriers break down when people pray together. I have seen people from warring countries in the same prayer meeting loving each other in Christ. Only the oneness of the faith, the solid belief in "Our Father," can do that.

Lord, thank you for believers in every part of the world.

Be informed about what God is doing elsewhere in the world. Pray for believers in other places who are likewise praying for you.

■ HOPE BRINGER

Col. 1:24-29: "To them God has chosen to make known among the Gentiles the glorious riches of this mystery, which is Christ in you, the hope of glory" (v. 27).

What is God's way of bringing hope to the hopeless? The answer is very personal: you are. How will God show himself to those who know nothing of him or who have been captured by secularism, materialism, atheism, humanism, agnosticism? God will use you. Christ in you is the hope of glory. Christ is our hope. When Christ is in you, you exemplify that hope. You are an ambassador of hope. You are the one to show the better side of life.

What are the riches of his glory? You are—Christ in you. You are the hope bringer. Redemption is gloriously rich, so eternal life is gloriously rich, and the message of hope you bring is gloriously rich.

Don't spend your years in what is temporal. Give your life to the ministry of hope bringing. Give to people what is eternal—hope in Christ. Be a hope bringer by living out the hope, "Christ in you."

Have you opened your life fully to Christ so he can rule in you and make you a hope bringer to this world that needs that hope?

Lord, live in me. Let me be a hope bringer. Help me to be so yielded that Christ is in me, and by seeing Christ in me people will see the hope of glory.

Whatever you do today, do it with the thought in mind, "I am a hope bringer."

STEPS TO PEACE WITH GOD

1. RECOGNIZE GOD'S PLAN—PEACE AND LIFE

The message you have read in this book stresses that God loves you and wants you to experience His peace and life.

The BIBLE says . . . *"For God loved the world so much that He gave His only Son, so that everyone who believes in Him may not die but have eternal life." John 3:16*

2. REALIZE OUR PROBLEM—SEPARATION

People choose to disobey God and go their own way. This results in separation from God.

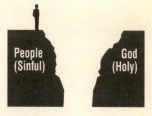

The BIBLE says . . . *"Everyone has sinned and is far away from God's saving presence." Romans 3:23*

3. RESPOND TO GOD'S REMEDY—CROSS OF CHRIST

God sent His Son to bridge the gap. Christ did this by paying the penalty of our sins when He died on the cross and rose from the grave.

The BIBLE says . . . *"But God has shown us how much He loves us—it was while we were still sinners that Christ died for us!" Romans 5:8*

4. RECEIVE GOD'S SON—LORD AND SAVIOR

You cross the bridge into God's family when you ask Christ to come into your life.

The BIBLE says . . . *"Some, however, did receive Him and believed in Him; so He gave them the right to become God's children." John 1:12*

THE INVITATION IS TO:
REPENT (turn from your sins) and by faith RECEIVE Jesus Christ into your heart and life and follow Him in obedience as your Lord and Savior.

PRAYER OF COMMITMENT
"Lord Jesus, I know I am a sinner. I believe You died for my sins. Right now, I turn from my sins and open the door of my heart and life. I receive You as my personal Lord and Savior. Thank You for saving me now. Amen."

If you want further help in the decision you have made, write to:
Billy Graham Evangelistic Association, P.O. Box 779, Minneapolis, MN 55440-0779